HIGHER EDUCATION FOR ALL?

HIGHER EDUCATION FOR ALL?

*Edited by Gordon Roderick
and Michael Stephens*

 The Falmer Press

35184

First published 1979

ISBN 0 905273 10 9

Jacket illustration by Jacky Thomas
Jacket design by Leonard Williams

Printed and bound in Hong Kong for

The Falmer Press
Falmer House
Barcombe, Lewes
Sussex BN8 5DL
England

Contents

Part Four: The Political Implications

Part Five: Conclusion

Editors' Acknowlegements

Our thanks to the contributors for their impeccable good manners in the face of our harassment, to the many unnamed individuals who provided information, advice, or typing skills, and to Miss Margaret Smith for her incomparable administrative-cum-secretarial aid.

Introduction

Gordon W. Roderick and Michael D. Stephens

For the first time since Plato mentioned the idea in the seventh book of *The Republic*, education for a majority of Western societies' citizens throughout their lives has become a serious debating point. Legislation is beginning to follow. For example, when passing Public Law 94–482 on 12 October 1976 the US Congress stated (Section 131):

1. accelerating social and technological change have had impact on the duration and quality of life;
2. the American people need lifelong learning to enable them to adjust to social, technological, political and economic changes;
3. lifelong learning has a role in developing the potential of all persons including improvement of their personal wellbeing, upgrading their work-place skills, and preparing them to participate in the civic, cultural, and political life of the Nation;
4. lifelong learning is important in meeting the needs of the growing number of older and retired persons;
5. learning takes place through formal and informal instruction, through educational programs conducted by public and private educational and other institutions and organizations, through independent study, and through the efforts of business, industry, and labor;
6. planning is necessary at the national, state, and local levels to assure effective use of existing resources in the light of changing characteristics and learning needs of the population;
7. more effective use should be made of the resources of the Nation's educational institutions in order to assist the people of the United States in the solution of community problems in areas such as housing, poverty, government, recreation, employment, youth opportunities, transportation, health, and land use; and
8. American society should have as a goal the availability of appropriate opportunities for lifelong learning for all its citizens without regard to restrictions of previous education or training, sex, age, handicapping condition, social or ethnic background, or economic circumstance.

It is against such national and international discussion that the future of higher education must be seen. As President Steven Muller stated at the Johns Hopkins University centennial celebrations in 1976:

> As complex a society as ours will continue to need to make higher education available to most citizens. We will still need the sophisticated skills in which the university offers training; we need citizens fully schooled in their culture; and we need research that advances knowledge and promotes reason. There is a question here, but it is not whether the university is needed, nor even whether it will be supported. The question is whether the university can respond effectively to *new* needs, to opportunities of an unprecedented kind.

To a certain extent the 'lifelong learning' debate has taken many of the higher education systems of the world by surprise. As recently as 1963 the United Kingdom's 'Higher Education Report' (HMSO Cmnd. 2154, The Robbins Report) could state (pp. 6–7):

> In our submission there are at least four objectives essential to any properly balanced system [of higher education].
>
> We begin with instruction in skills suitable to play a part in the general division of labour. We put this first, not because we regard it as the most important, but because we think that it is sometimes ignored or undervalued. Confucius said in the Analects that it was not easy to find a man who had studied for three years without aiming at pay. We deceive ourselves if we claim that more than a small fraction of students in institutions of higher education would be where they are if there were no significance for their future careers in what they hear and read; and it is a mistake to suppose that there is anything discreditable in this. Certainly this was not the attitude of the past: the ancient universities of Europe were founded to promote the training of the clergy, doctors and lawyers; and though at times there may have been many who attended for the pursuit of pure knowledge or of pleasure, they must surely have been a minority. And it must be recognised that in our own times, progress – and particularly the maintenance of a competitive position – depends to a much greater extent than ever before on skills demanding special training. A good general education, valuable though it may be, is frequently less than we need to solve many of our most pressing problems.
>
> But, secondly, while emphasising that there is no betrayal of

values when institutions of higher education teach what will be of some practical use, we must postulate that what is taught should be taught in such a way as to promote the general powers of the mind. The aim should be to produce not mere specialists but rather cultivated men and women. And it is the distinguishing characteristic of a healthy higher education that, even where it is concerned with practical techniques, it imparts them on a plane of generality that makes possible their application to many problems – to find the one in the many, the general characteristic in the collection of particulars. It is this that the world of affairs demands of the world of learning. And it is this, and not conformity with traditional categories, that furnishes the criterion of what institutions of higher education may properly teach.

Thirdly, we must name the advancement of learning. There are controversial issues here concerning the balance between teaching and research in the various institutions of higher education and the distribution of research between these institutions and other bodies. We shall deal with these later. But the search for truth is an essential function of institutions of higher education and the process of education is itself most vital when it partakes of the nature of discovery. It would be untrue to suggest that the advancement of knowledge has been or ever will be wholly dependent on universities and other institutions of higher education. But the world, not higher education alone, will suffer if ever they cease to regard it as one of their main functions.

Finally, there is a function that is more difficult to describe concisely, but that is none the less fundamental: the transmission of a common culture and common standards of citizenship. By this we do not mean the forcing of all individuality into a common mould: that would be the negation of higher education as we conceive it. But we believe that it is a proper function of higher education, as of education in schools, to provide in partnership with the family that background of culture and social habit upon which a healthy society depends. This function, important at all times, is perhaps especially important in an age that has set for itself the ideal of equality of opportunity. It is not merely by providing places for students from all classes that this ideal will be achieved, but also by providing, in the atmosphere of the institutions in which the students live and work, influences that in some measure compensate for any inequalities of home background. These influences are not limited to the student population. Universities and colleges have an important role to play in the general cultural life of the communities in which they are situated.

. By the 1970s the flood of official reports (e.g. Alberta's 'A Choice of Futures' [1972], Manitoba's 'Task Force on Post-Secondary Education' [1972], Ontario's Wright Report [1972], UNESCO's 'Learning To Be' [1973]) all had in common the central theme of planning for education throughout a citizen's life. Whereas the Robbins Report assumed that the main role of institutions of higher education would be to educate an increasing percentage of those in late adolescence, by 1977 the United Kingdom's Secretary of State for Education and Science, Shirley Williams, in a lecture on 'Robbins plus 20: which way for higher education?' (*The Times Higher Education Supplement*, 9 December 1977) was pointing out that:

> *The concept of continuing or recurrent education is gaining ground.* Increasingly we realize that education and training cannot be met wholly in school and immediate post-school provision. Mature adults need to be able to return to education and training throughout life for various reasons (women picking up careers again after raising their families, mature students changing careers because of redundancy or shifts in industrial employment patterns, need to update technical and professional competence). Post-school education and training is now seen as a continuum permitting many combinations of mode of attendance, subject areas, levels of study according to students' needs and motivation. What have hitherto been administratively convenient bundles of provision no longer have rigid boundaries. We need to think in a student-centred rather than an institution-centred way.

Particularly in higher education the idea of a once-for-all education is no longer viable. Change, whether technological, economic or social, is too rapid to leave unchallenged the apprenticeship model of education. In a society where the knowledge of those now graduating from a university's medical school has already become outdated compared to that received by the first year students, higher education cannot do other than accept a central philosophy of lifelong education. 'The notion that a man can live his life-span equipped with a store of knowledge acquired during his formal school-days is no longer acceptable. The adaptability needed to develop one's true potential, especially in a rapidly changing society, must be nurtured throughout one's life-time by systematic adult education' (Irish Ministry of Education, 1973). Those with the most 'learning' from the 'front-end model', such as university graduates, will find themselves in the most exposed position if only because they have more 'knowledge' to become dated.

Any discussion of a system of higher education for all must have as its foundation the assumption that lifelong education is its framework. As Schwartz (1977) has pointed out regarding one area of higher education: 'The university is thus seen as an ideal meeting point of initial and continuing education, a segment of the permanent education system admitting and placing side by side those who are resuming studies and those who have just left secondary school.'

There are, of course, powerful forces against recognizing lifelong education as a priority. The high cost of the present system of initial education makes the demand for extra resources for continuing education unpopular. The obvious answer to this problem, namely to switch resources from child- and adolescent-centred education, has been countered by the education lobby's ability to convince the public that school education still suffers limitations because of a lack of resources. Those with above average educational qualification resist what they often see as the threatening suggestion that they need to return regularly for requalification. Everyone pays lip service to recognizing an ever increasing rate of creation of new knowledge, but few are willing to acknowledge their own knowledge obsolescence.

The vested interest in, and complexity of, the initial education system make change which is other than cosmetic difficult to achieve. The 'system' may be willing to agree to everyone eventually spending the years from eighteen to twenty-one in full-time education, but it does not question the basis of the present content and organization of higher education. We never seem to get to grips with the issues of fundamental change. For example, the Open University Report of the Committee on Continuing Education, which was published in the United Kingdom in December 1976, was a document greatly to be welcomed. But, as the following recommendations (p. 7) illustrate, little is questioned in the traditional higher education format:

(iii) every effort to preserve access for the largest possible number of students in any programme of continuing education, recognizing that the fees charged to the student are a major factor in determining access. *Paragraph 112*

(iv) moves towards positive discrimination in favour of those adults who have not benefited from a mandatory award previously, and those who are not eligible under the recommendation on paid educational leave; and in addition the keeping of fees for continuing education as low as possible and their reduction for those who have been given less by the educational system so far. *Paragraph 26*

(v) efforts to persuade the government to fulfil its undertaking to the International Labour Organization convention on paid educational leave. *Paragraph 25*

(vi) action in concert with other appropriate bodies to secure an adequate provision of educational facilities and allowances for the disabled adult. *Paragraph 82*

(vii) the integrated development and use of the library services, both public and in educational institutions such as universities, polytechnics and colleges, as part of a general improvement of this national resource in continuing education. *Paragraph 39*

(viii) pressure for a considerable increase in time for educational broadcasting, and particularly for continuing education.
Paragraph 88

(ix) a sustained analysis, from the outset of developments, of the problems of copyright, contracts, compatibility of technical equipment, editorial responsibility and other operational and legal problems. *Paragraph 46*

(x) any national moves designed to increase the opportunities for part-time postgraduates to study at universities in the United Kingdom. *Paragraph 52*

As Richards (1975) commented of a previous document:

To me one of the most surprising aspects of the Robbins Report was the complete lack of any suggestion that universities should move away one iota from their accepted pattern of three-year courses for 18 year old school-leavers, coupled with one-year and three-year post-graduate programmes leading to masters and doctors degrees. At no point did they suggest that this was only one of the many educational frameworks which might be needed in the future, and that three years was rather a long unit of time upon which to base a young student's decision whether or not he wanted to continue with some form of tertiary education, especially in view of the rather poor financial reward for such effort, and the often excessive narrowness of so many of the courses of study available to him. Mrs. Thatcher, in her 1972 White Paper, took up the concept of a two-year Dip.H.E. as a staging post in a longer educational process, but this was widely interpreted as a means of obtaining education 'on the cheap'.

Of even greater significance than the changing of the structures of higher education programmes is to debate the content. Unfortunately in the higher education for all discussions, Western society is still mainly at the 'more of the same' stage. The Open University, for example, is often seen as a way of providing a traditional higher education by part-time (and cheaper) means, not as a route to a 'new' higher education.

In 1974 American institutions of higher education awarded 316,000 master's degrees and 35,000 doctoral degrees. By 1981–2 the Robbins Report's projected figure of 560,000 places in the United Kingdom's higher education sector for 1980–1 may be reached. Between 1960 and 1970 the number of Hungarian universities and colleges rose from 43 to 74. By 1977 the law faculty of the University of Athens had 25,000 students. In the last forty years the number of female university teachers in Yugoslavia has risen by 191 times. There can be no doubt that in virtually all countries of the world higher education has seen a remarkable growth in numbers. What has been lacking is a healthy questioning of the traditional models. Higher education has not been notable for its programme innovation. As the Dutch have discovered (Dutch Ministry of Education and Science, 1975):

The present objectives of the universities and higher vocational institutes are narrowly interpreted at the moment. The text of the objectives, notably that in the University Education Act, allows far more freedom. But the spirit of the times has long encouraged over-specialisation. Either we follow scientific developments, as in the universities, or we follow the increasing professionalism in society, as in both the universities and the higher vocational institutes.

The spirit of the times is changing, however. Professional speciali-sation in our society, especially is open to doubt. Are we not losing the balance between this and democratic co-determination, to the detriment of the latter? Are not efforts towards professionalisation, in all sectors of the community, being exaggerated? These are fundamental questions which are important in themselves and also as regards the measure of professionalism that should be demanded of students.

Elite institutions, of which the universities are the prime examples, usually fight change the hardest. Change may lead to loss of status and attendant privileges. As a result many countries, faced with a pressing need for a 'different' higher education system to the traditional and inherited, have created or expanded institutions parallel to the universities. To take

Table 1. *Advanced courses in public sector institutions: number of institutions in 1981 and related numbers of students 1975–6 (England and Wales)*[1]

		Expected pattern of institutions 1981	Student numbers 1975–6			
	Type	No.	Full-time	Sandwich	Part-time	Evening
Polytechnics	—	30	78,153[2]	30,233[2]	37,943[2]	16,344[2]
Other institutions						
(i) with over 90 per cent advanced work:						
	Former colleges of education, free-standing or amalgamated with other colleges	57	53,575	239	2,165	966
	Specialist colleges[5]	7	3,200	—	41	49
	Other colleges	3	604	—	19	—
(ii) with between 30 per cent and 90 per cent advanced work:						
	Former colleges of education amalgamated with other colleges	18	17,885	2,029	9,654	4,318
	Specialist colleges[4]	25	4,238	814	40	—
	Other colleges	14	4,876	1,475	6,847	3,417
(iii) with less than 30 per cent advanced work:						
	Former colleges of education amalgamated with other colleges	2	1,322	10	668	305
	Specialist colleges[4]	7	51	142	—	4
	Other colleges: with full-time or sandwich students	96	5,085	3,188	20,028	8,191
	with no full-time or sandwich students	159	—	—	10,265	4,436
Total		418	168,989[3]	38,130[3]	87,670	38,030

[1] This table represents the position as forecast in autumn 1976 and takes no account of further changes which may result from the Secretary of State's proposals of 24 January 1977.

[2] These figures include students at colleges of education expected to merge with polytechnics by 1981.

[3] This table excludes those colleges which are to become part of the university sector or to close.

[4] Including colleges of art and design, music, drama and agriculture.

For further debate of projected figures for the United Kingdom see the DES Discussion Document, 'Higher Education into the 1990s', London 1978.

Source: Department of Education and Science 'Report of Education, No. 90' May 1977.

England and Wales as a case study the growth in non-university higher education has been remarkable (Table 1).

In 1975–6 the public sector had an estimated 216,000 full-time and sandwich students whereas the universities had 223,000. The 1981–2 figure for higher education implied a 39 per cent growth in advanced further education, mainly in the polytechnics, and a 14 per cent growth in the university sector.

The polytechnics have not produced the new thinking in the higher education of England and Wales that might have been expected of them. They have largely emulated the powerful university model. It could be suggested that if the polytechnics were renamed 'universities' they would fit into the category without any difficulty.

Despite the strong similarity between the provision of the university sector and that of the polytechnics in some areas, such as qualifications by part-time study, the latter have been more adventurous.

The Polytechnic of Central London illustrates such innovation well. By 1977 the Polytechnic had over 100 part-time courses of at least thirty weeks' duration and was launching new part-time programmes at both undergraduate and postgraduate level. In few universities, the notable exceptions being Birkbeck College, the Open University, and some modest provision at Hull, are first degrees by part-time study provided. The polytechnics' record has been far more honourable.

The parallel short courses programme at the Polytechnic of Central London has grown from 1,063 enrolments in 1971–2 to 9,613 in 1976–7. The major objectives of the programme have been listed as:
1. Enlarging and up-dating of expertise for those employed in professional, managerial and specialist work.
2. Propagation of new knowledge and application of existing knowledge to new and unfamiliar fields.
3. Discussion of the major social, economic, legal and environmental issues of the day.
4. Service to the community, with special reference to teachers and pupils, local and central government, industry and commerce, and individual citizens.
5. Staff development within the Polytechnic and increased opportunities for job-satisfaction.
Pro-Rector David Liston writes further:

> Short courses leading neither to degrees nor diplomas are no new feature of the British educational scene. Extra-mural and other Departments of Universities and Polytechnics have offered this type

of programme to supplement their more formal degree, professional and qualifying courses. Similarly Colleges of Further Education, Liberal Arts and Adult Education have all within their particular areas of expertise sought through short-course programmes to meet a diverse range of local and regional educational and social interests. In this general field, the short-course activity at PCL is quite distinctive and in some ways a world leader. In the first instance, the number of participants is very large. Secondly, the courses are for the most part financially self-supporting, with administration, publicity, class materials and the cost of visiting lecturers all paid for out of course fees. The fees themselves are kept as low as possible and are related to the target audience for each individual course. They range from £28 per day for open management courses for middle and senior executives, to 50p for sixth formers attending one-day pupil-teacher courses in biology and other aspects of life sciences.

Thirdly, a high proportion of the courses are held in evenings, at weekends and in vacation, thus multiplying the productivity of the Institution and utilising to what must be an unprecedented extent costly buildings and facilities located in the heart of Central London.

Finally, in spite of the essentially entrepreneurial approach to marketing and financing, short courses at PCL are essentially a mainstream educational activity. Each of the eight Schools has its own short-course generator, all of them members of the academic staff, and most of them with current teaching responsibilities on long courses as well as short. Short-course programmes are approved by the School Board, in some cases through a specially constituted Continuing Education Committee.

The subject matter of the courses is broadly related either to the main academic interests of the School or to the particular specialism of individual members of staff. They are directed variously at the propagation of new knowledge, at the application of existing knowledge to new and unfamiliar areas, and increasingly at the study of the great social, economic, legal and environmental issues of the day.

The Polytechnic of Central London is a pacemaker in these areas of innovation and cannot be taken as typical of the whole of the polytechnic sector of British higher education.

It would therefore seem likely that British higher education may be willing to discuss continued expansion but within the context of a 'traditional' set of syllabuses. With this will go closer co-ordination between the different sectors as proposed in the Report of the Working Group on the

Management of Higher Education in the Maintained Sector (Cmnd. 7130, HMSO 1978).

Many of the above themes have been summarised by Professor Jan Kluczynski, Director of the Institute of Science Policy and Higher Education in Warsaw (Kluczynski, 1976):

> *First*, in view of the expected limits in the resources of economic growth, it will be necessary to adapt university education to the new conditions.
>
> *Second*, in time, the social need for wide access to education may also apply to higher education. It is necessary, therefore, to start to look for ways which would make mass schooling at a higher and semi-higher level possible. In fact, an improvement in the standard of living, with a simultaneous increase in free time, will increase people's cultural and educational aspirations during their whole life time, and this need will also concern the higher education institutions.
>
> *Third*, the development of science and technology brings about radical changes in the choice of content and methods in all types of education. The scientific-technological revolution results in a need for specialized personnel who have a high level of general education. To educate an individual who is active, innovation-minded and ready to improve his professional skills – this should be the task of an educational system.
>
> *Fourth*, the educational system is an important factor in the process of developing a person's personality and abilities; at the same time, however, this is only the beginning of the continuing process of life-long education. The rapid development of science and technology leads to changes in the nature and content of labour and this will always require new qualifications which will have to be improved continuously during the professional life. This type of educational model will require permanent improvement and even professional re-training. Therefore the needs for life-long education should be taken into consideration when planning the educational system as a whole and also in the educational activities undertaken by employers.
>
> *Fifth*, the important rôle of science in implementing socio-economic progress will make it necessary to integrate higher education in the research and development system in such a way as to take advantage of the potential for research existing in higher education institutions.
>
> *Sixth*, in a modern higher education system it will be necessary to include students more extensively in the scientific research pro-

gramme carried out by the institutions of higher learning. This type of research will, at the same time, be a new form of university training.

Seventh, the future socio-political and cultural development of the nation is conditioned by the level of education of society as a whole, by its readiness for innovation and by the possibility of adaptation to changing tasks and functions. So far, discussion on the concept of the higher education institution, in relation to the abilities and knowledge of the secondary school graduates applying for admission to higher education, has raised the question of whether it would not be necessary for them to undertake preparation courses in the first stage of their higher education training. Other important questions arise in connection with how to reconcile the present system with the proposed individualization of education, the greater participation of students in research work, and other tasks which face many national education systems.

Professor Kluczynski was Secretary to the Committee which prepared the 1973 'Report on the State of Education in Poland'. His emphases confirm the international nature of the points raised by the movement in the more affluent countries towards some form of higher education for all.

The debate in Sweden has moved a stage further than in most countries. The U68 proposals (see also Chapter 10) made an assumption that there would eventually be some sort of 'higher education' for almost everyone, but that higher education would become 'different' because of mass access. As Bergendal (1977) pointed out: 'The abstract, theoretical character of traditional university studies is not attractive to everyone'.

In the final Report of UNESCO's Committee of Experts on Post-Secondary Education for Persons Gainfully Employed (1976) at least one practical aspect of universal higher education was tackled in the recommendation that:

> The timing of post-secondary education during a person's career should be a function of his occupational objectives, his interests, needs and personal abilities in the area of general, social and civic education, and should not generally be limited to any specific time frame. There are, however, critical times for education associated with re-training through a person's lifetime.

It would seem likely that such organizational points will be dealt with first as they raise less complex issues than do perhaps more fundamental debates like, 'What are the higher education requirements of the least able members of the country's population and how can they be met?'. In the final stages of debating the Swedish higher education reforms of 1977 it was hoped that such concepts as 'need' could be effectively met by a highly decentralized higher education system so that the variety of opinions and options could be maximized in their influence on syllabuses.

However, the decision to create a system of higher education for all is basically a political one. This has been pointed out over the creation of the previously mentioned binary system of higher education in England and Wales (Pedley, 1977). Following the Robbins Report of 1963 the new Labour Government of 1964 had three courses of action:

> The first was to accept the Robbins recommendations as they stood and so to entrust the main development of higher education, for many years ahead, to self-governing institutions, bearing in mind that the nature of such development would greatly influence the character of all the other sectors of education. Toby Weaver, at the time deputy secretary at DES, has since stated that if all the Robbins proposals had been carried out, 88 per cent of all higher-education students would have been in autonomous institutions and a depressed 12 per cent elsewhere.

> The second was the course chosen, that of compromise: to restrict the further enlargement of the autonomous sector by gently squeezing the universities and preventing them from enlarging their share of the pool of ability, while building alongside them an alternative structure, under public control, which could ensure at any rate that the most urgent national needs would be met.

> The third course, a thorough review of the whole field of post-school education, which would have had in mind the merging of existing universities in a unified structure under effective public control, and the challenging and possible changing of many of their present assumptions and practices, demanded courage of a high order. If it was considered at all at that time – and we have had no firm intimation to this effect – it must have been dismissed as impractical (as Crosland later dismissed it), involving delays in expansion which the nation could not afford and would not tolerate. On the other hand exposition of a genuinely comprehensive policy for higher education, with the declared intention to work towards it, would have preserved credit among many educationists and others who (as things turned out) felt betrayed by what seemed to them an obvious reversion to the mistaken attitudes of 1945.

The chapters that follow this introduction come within the framework of 'a thorough review of the whole field of post-school education'. Although authorities in a number of disciplines such as economics, or sociology, or political science, have been invited to contribute, there are many common themes, notably in the area of definition, e.g. what is higher education, or what is the nature of the education process?

As might be expected, the broad ranging theme of higher education for everyone produces a welter of ideas but, perhaps more surprisingly, an equal abundance of examples and existing or emerging models. To the British reader what is bad for the ego is to realize how much has been written on the subject and how far many other countries have moved further along the road to fulfilling mass higher education, if not universal higher education.

Perhaps the whole issue of higher education for all can be bluntly summarized by a passage in a recent publication (OECD 1977):

> The very strong individual demand for higher education, which is now spreading among adults, continues in large measure to be governed by the social and economic status that it has acquired. The sum total of these demands is still rising. Although its composition changes in relation to students' perceptions of career prospects in different occupations, the total demand for higher education appears to be autonomous and not conditioned by specific employment prospects. It shows little sign of being contained by or adapting itself to the currently and prospectively limited and uncertain overall employment prospects for graduates, especially in the public sector, including teaching, which until recently has absorbed a very high proportion of them. A central problem is to what extent and by what means this demand can be satisfied: on one hand it is recognized that higher education has a vital contribution to make to economic development and employment and that its cultural objectives are specially important: yet on the other hand it has to be borne in mind that there are limitations on resources, that other levels of education have competing claims, and that many countries are concerned to provide a more equitable access to education within society.

If all other factors are ignored, what is left is the problem of whether higher education for all can be funded and, if we can afford it, whether it can meet the educational needs of everyone. The Department of Education and Science's Discussion Document 'Higher Education into the 1990s' issued in London in February 1978 demonstrated that the United Kingdom is still debating the move from an elitist to a mass higher education system.

The Model E discussed, however, did include such important elements as 'recurrent education for mature students', but the flavour of the writing suggested that London will not be the pacemaker in 'higher education for all' that Stockholm, or Ottawa, or Washington DC is.

To finish on an encouraging note it is worth quoting the Minister of State Gordon Oakes (*The Times Higher Education Supplement*, 26 May 1978) on North Sea oil revenue:

> Without a shadow of a doubt the best possible focus for an investment in this area is provided by the education service. And when I say education, I mean predominantly higher and further education, together with the overlapping field of research.
>
> Education and research, besides being indisputably good things in their own right, deserve the lion's share of investment from our North Sea bonus strictly on their own merits, possessing as they do the capacity to raise our national level of efficiency – and therefore also our economic viability – and help put it on a much more permanent basis. I believe it represents an investment we simply cannot afford *not* to make.

References

Adult Education in Ireland: a Report of a Committee appointed by the Minister of Education, Dublin 1973, p. 4.

Contours of a Future Education System in the Netherlands, Ministry of Education and Science, The Hague 1975, p. 147.

Education and Working Life, Organisation for Economic Co-operation and Development, Paris 1977, pp. 38–9.

BERGENDAL, G. (1977) *Higher Education and Manpower Planning in Sweden*. Stockholm. The National Board of Universities and Colleges.

KLUCZYNSKI, J. 'Higher Education – How Will It Develop?' in *Higher Education in Europe* July–October 1976, pp. 38–9.

PEDLEY, R. (1977) *Towards the Comprehensive University*, Macmillan, pp. 43–4.

RICHARDS, E. J. (1975) *Adult Education: a Challenge to All* University College, Cardiff.

SCHWARTZ, B. (1977) 'Secondary and Tertiary Education' in *Work of Consolidation of the Evaluation of Pilot Experiments in the Permanent Education Field*, Council of Europe, Strasbourg.

PART ONE

The Academic Implications

1. The Concept of Higher Education for All Explored

Kenneth Lawson

One of the dominant trends in education throughout much of this century has been the movement towards greater equality in education. It is almost inevitable therefore that following the achievement in Britain of universal secondary education, attention should turn towards the idea of higher education for all. The term 'universal higher education' has been used in the United States; Sweden has within the last few years made University education more widely available, while in Britain the topic is appearing in a number of places and a book has appeared recently under the title of *Towards The Comprehensive University* (Pedley 1977). Higher education which has long appeared as an élitist concept is being re-examined, criticized and reformulated in a more popular egalitarian form.

It should be said straightway that the idea of 'universal higher education' is a very attractive concept and the debate about its desirability coincides nicely with discussions about the need for higher education institutions to concern themselves more with the practical problems of the work-a-day world of industry and commerce and with the many pressing problems facing society. In the face of criticism about the alleged lack of 'relevance' in education generally, it is very difficult for such issues to be ignored and there are good social and economic reasons for considering the possibility of more widespread higher education and the related question of greater everyday relevance of education.

However, new ideas are not necessarily wholly good and it might be a mistake to accept them uncritically without trying to establish what they might mean, and what their theoretical and practical implications might be. My purpose therefore is to consider some of the possible implications of the concept of 'universal higher education' and to outline a number of issues which the idea seems to raise. In particular I shall consider what 'universal higher education' might be taken to mean and discuss what seem to be implications for the curriculum of higher education. In doing so I hope to raise questions connected with the problem of motivating people to engage in higher education and with the closely related issue of the practical relevance of education.

On the face of it there might seem to be no problem raised by the idea

27

of 'higher education for all' beyond the practical problem of providing the necessary resources with which to make the idea a reality. It should be apparent however that after more than thirty years of universal secondary education we still seem to be unclear about the nature of secondary education on a mass scale for all levels of ability. There is still argument about the content, the methodology and the organization of secondary education, which suggests that an educational slogan does not necessarily translate easily into an educational policy. If we are proclaiming the right to higher education for all, what have we in mind?

An equal right or an equal education?

On its narrowest interpretation the idea of universal higher education might imply no more than the establishment of an equal right of access to the resources of higher education but, as Mary Warnock has reminded us, this is by no means the same as a right to equal access (Warnock, 1977). We have an equal right of access to the resources of the National Health Service but the resources placed at an individual's disposal vary according to the diagnosis of his illness. An equal right to education does not entail either equality in the kind of education or in its duration, and a further set of decisions is required in order to establish exactly what each individual should have. Do we seek the same kind of higher education and for the same duration for every adult in the population? If so, is it a feasible policy? If this is not what is intended, what range of educational opportunities and processes might have to be provided in order to cater for the adult population and what are to be the criteria for determining the limits of what is to count as a 'higher education'? It might be possible to provide a post-school education for all, but whether or not all 'post-school education' can count as 'higher education' is doubtful.

The problem of motivation and the nature of higher education

On general grounds there appears to be a case for arguing that the establishment of an equal right to higher education is not sufficient to ensure that the right will be exercised equally and a conventionally conceived curriculum of higher education seems unlikely to have universal appeal. Adult education is already available to most people but not everyone chooses to engage in it, partly because there are many who do not recognize or admit its relevance to them.

The higher education sector already embraces a wide range of courses within a variety of institutions. There is no single level of higher education either in the universities or elsewhere. It might be realistic to cater for many more adults within the present institutional and curricular framework but past experience and reflection upon the nature of what we call 'higher education' suggests that a considerable modification of that concept might be necessary in order to attract the total adult population.

How far the concept of 'higher education' can be modified without significant loss of meaning is both a theoretical and a practical question the consequences of which might be far reaching, and there may be a case for retaining a non-popular non-egalitarian sector of higher education, properly so-called, with some new pattern of popular education under such appellation as 'continuing' or 'further' or 'adult' education.

Whether or not the term 'higher education' should be retained to refer to some form of 'mass' post-school education might seem to be no more than a semantic issue but concepts have a descriptive connotation which is indicative of characteristics which we expect to find in areas to which the concept is applied. It is not for example unimportant whether a form of political organization shall be called 'democratic'. Certain things are expected of this title and it describes as well as names. The same may be said of 'higher education'.

We must consider in a moment what are the characteristics of 'higher education', but first it might be worth considering why the term has more appeal than other forms of education which might be made more widely available.

Part of the appeal probably derives from the social status traditionally given to 'higher education'. It has a well established élitist image and it still tends to provide routes to higher-status jobs. 'Higher' is seen in terms of status instead of being located in a more neutral way at the top of an educational hierarchy which distinguishes between different forms of education, but which need not be regarded as 'better'. That some are seen to be 'better' indicates the social values with which they are imbued. If the special features which identify 'higher education' indicate educational differences a conceptual distinction may be drawn. It might then be urged that 'higher' refers to a logically higher or more abstract form of education. It can be regarded as 'better' only if we are prepared for example to argue that 'education' is better than 'training' whereas the two have their respective places and are concepts which indicate different functions, each of value in its place. Hammers are only better than screw-drivers if we are driving nails or breaking coal.

If we can separate the idea of 'higher education' from its social connotations it might be possible to see its place within a system of education more clearly. If it has a particular place which can be detached from social status, its egalitarian appeal might be reduced. It is not unjust because some people train as teachers, others as engineers and some as mechanics. Injustice in these matters arises from the processes by which selection is made. There might be a case to be made for some people engaging in higher education and others doing something different rather than attempt to modify beyond acceptable limits what we mean by 'higher education', in an attempt to cater comprehensively for everyone. Before any egalitarian arguments are allowed to intrude we should consider how far higher education is appropriate to the majority of people because only when such questions have been answered does it make sense to devise ways of making higher education more widely available. We might conclude that equity requires that access to higher education shall not be available only to a privileged minority and that more open access and more equal right of access are the central issues rather than an education of the same kind for everyone.

In trying to establish the most appropriate response to the idea of universal higher education it must be stressed that the arguments used are about the relevance of various forms of education to the situations in which people find themselves. The arguments about limited pools of ability as a significant limitation to the availability of higher education are not regarded as important. If someone chooses to engage in higher education there might be good reason for letting him attempt it. My concern is with those people who do not see higher education as relevant and who may well be correct in their judgement. A universal system of higher education which many do not want would be a sham and a waste of resources which might otherwise be diverted to kinds of education which do have more popular appeal and relevance. Nevertheless we are prejudging the issue by assuming that higher education might not have general appeal and it becomes necessary at this stage to define more precisely what is meant by 'higher education' and this involves identifying some of the major characteristics associated with the concept. We then return to some of the problems which might arise from attempts to introduce universal higher education. Some of these problems are also inherent in any attempt to re-orientate higher education more specifically to the demands of industry and society: the belief that this should be attempted appears to be gaining ground and is a current area of debate. This debate takes education more directly into the field of politics where educational decisions become overlaid with political judgements and up to a point it is both inevitable and desirable that this should be so. Education both reflects and influences society and educators cannot expect to make decisions which influence and try to change people and also make demands upon public resources without having to justify their actions. In the ensuing debate on what educators wish to do, conflicting aims and interests will inevitably arise. At some point, however, those who are involved in education must determine the limits beyond which they cannot yield to political pressure and popular demand except by compromising their central values. Educators might have no right in a democracy to defend their position at all costs, but they have a duty to draw attention to the possible consequences of being forced to make radical changes. Some changes are desirable but others might not be and it is important to attempt to identify what the critical areas might be.

Some of the issues have been discussed recently in the editorial of *Higher Education Review* Summer 1977. Reference is made there to the pressures to direct education more specifically towards industry and society and the task which is identified is that of relating economic, industrial and social problems to the problems of the student, the latter being the educators' primary concern. It is suggested that in relating these two sets of problems, a new kind of curriculum is likely to emerge and it will be determined by what students need in a social context. Such a statement seems admirably suited to a discussion on the possibility of establishing universal higher education and it becomes more significant when the conclusion is drawn that 'knowledge will no longer be the dominant feature of higher education'.

Such a change of emphasis would represent a major challenge to the traditional view of higher education and it is in this challenge that the central defining characteristic of 'higher education' is clearly seen.

The concept and purpose of higher education

One way of identifying higher education is illustrated in the Robbins Report which stresses the level of generality which is expected in contrast to other forms of education, but the main feature may be seen in the clear orientation towards knowledge, as contained in the various academic disciplines. It is from this knowledge alone that higher education derives its rationale, its curriculum and its values. What is taught may be determined partly by reference to the demands of various professions as is the case with, say, teacher education and the education of doctors and engineers. But although the general area of the curriculum is selected with practical outcomes in mind, the details of the curriculum tend to be dominated by the structure of knowledge within the disciplines. Higher education is centrally concerned with initiation into the frameworks of knowledge, into the associated concepts, methods and values. This clearly does not exclude the possibility of higher education being pursued with instrumental aims in mind but such aims do not determine the character of higher education. Curriculum decisions are made in the light of educational values rather than externally imposed aims. How valid is such a view in the face of the pressures now being exerted?

One can agree that a balance between society and its problems and the values of higher education is desirable and it would be difficult to insist upon a rigid defence of the ivory tower. The question is more appropriately phrased in terms of how much emphasis there should be in one direction or the other. How far can we meet the demands of society while retaining a recognizable concept of 'higher education' and how far should those demands be met?

If it is argued that knowledge-oriented higher education is important and should be defended, then there are implications for the idea of universal higher education. To what extent can higher education be seen as relevant to most people if it is to remain knowledge-based? Can we modify higher education and move towards, say, a problem- and career-oriented curriculum in order to attract more people to it, or might it be more appropriate to discard the idea of universal *higher* education and turn instead to concepts such as 'continuing', 'recurrent' or 'adult' education?

In order to suggest answers to such questions it might help to consider how higher education can be and is already related to the requirements of work. This will help to indicate the limits to the extent to which change might be possible and desirable.

The kinds of work to which higher education is most directly relevant are in fields where academic knowledge is used extensively and the clearest case is the teaching of academic subjects. It is often said that university lecturers train more university lecturers and this is what higher education is best fitted to do. There are other kinds of jobs in such fields as chemistry, engineering, architecture and so on where the knowledge and understanding derived from a study of academic subjects can be drawn upon to a greater or a lesser extent. Such jobs are those with a considerable theoretical component and which draw upon principles and generalizations. But even in such work many lower level skills are needed and practical 'know-how' and what can be called 'recipe knowledge' are called for. It is partly a recognition of this fact which creates dissatisfaction in areas such as teacher education which the tension between the demands of academic subjects and the desire for more practical training are felt.

Even in fields where academic knowledge is most directly seen to be relevant it is not easy to define or identify the relationship between theory and practice and if improved performance is the major goal it can be difficult to assess the influence of education upon performance. 'Understanding' and 'insight' do not make a precisely measurable contribution.

Moreover there are many kinds of work where general understanding might in some sense produce 'better people' but has only marginal influence, if any, upon performance.

It is in the marginal cases that higher education is difficult to justify instrumentally and the majority of people may well be marginal in this sense. This is not to say that they should not receive a higher education but it has to be justifiable on some other grounds than its vocational relevance and its contribution to the economy.

In summary we can say that higher education has practical everyday relevance in proportion to the logical relationship between academic knowledge and the tasks involved and where the problems to be solved are definable in the categories of academic disciplines. Social and economic problems are definable in the categories of social science and economics, political science and history define political problems and the various sciences define technological problems. There would be no problems of chemistry without the science of chemistry and pre-scientific man saw only inexplicable mysteries, if he saw them at all, until the categories of science helped to formulate problems and to provide solutions.

A major function of higher education is on this view the transmission of concepts, methods, and validated knowledge, but associated with this is the process of evaluation and development of the disciplines themselves. If the disciplines are regarded as the public languages which help us to categorize and communicate our experience they require constant refinement and revision and how this is to be carried out is arguable. Traditionally the process of refinement and development of an academic discipline is undertaken in the light of criteria internal to the discipline and of problems created by the extension of knowledge within it. One set of questions leads to a further set of questions and the answers to questions in turn raise further problems.

It is argued that practical and external problems should provide the criteria by which to determine the direction of development of a discipline. Industry and society, it might be said, should generate the questions for academics and researchers to solve. In practice an interplay between the outside world and the academic domain helps to order research priorities as in cases where there is a demand for new technologies, sources of power and so on. But without the categories and their demands it is difficult to imagine how the practical problems could be foreseen or defined. Quite literally, new polymers could not be asked for in industry without the science which first conceived and produced them.

The proliferation of knowledge for the sake of knowledge might be criticized as being wasteful and for producing an unmanageable 'knowledge explosion' but it might be unwise to set limits in advance to the knowledge which is generated. Higher education plays a vital part in this process by training newcomers to the field and by stimulating scholarship and research.

Because of these functions higher education has a central role in our culture and it is a very specialized role. Not everyone would find it congenial to be educated with such purposes in mind and we are led to ask whether higher education in this specialized sense should be diluted in order to satisfy egalitarian notions. There appears to be a strong case for maintaining something like the present system based upon the idea of knowledge-centred education and it is the conditions of access which require scrutiny, not the development of a 'comprehensive' curriculum for a mass audience. Such a curriculum might have a place but not under the title of 'higher education'.

Liberal education and higher education

One conclusion that can be drawn from the discussion is that 'mass' post-school education should be varied and that it might be a serious mistake to concentrate too exclusively upon 'higher education for all'. There is a need for a post-school system with a variety of educational opportunities ranging from low-level skills training to sophisticated higher education on the model which has been described. What justice and equality require is flexibility which enables those who want education to select according to the needs of the moment. They should not be irrevocably committed to one type of education. Graduates from higher education might require low-level skills while others who have already acquired these might on occasion move into more sophisticated and theoretical areas either in relation to their work or for reasons connected with political life, leisure interests and so on. A policy of universal higher education rigidly conceived might well obscure the need for a more flexible structure.

There is perhaps one more possibility to be considered and that is the establishment of a comprehensive liberal education at some level short of 'higher education'. The problem of motivation would still be present but so would the curriculum problems. Simply expressed, the latter have to do with the content, the duration and the depth of study which would be desirable and worthwhile. There might be no single answer and in order to achieve equal results in educational terms, disproportionate resources may be required with positive discrimination for less well-endowed or less experienced students. In general terms, there are the questions of 'how much' and 'what kind of curriculum' to be considered.

A liberal education can be justified on the grounds that it develops autonomous thinking by providing the apparatus of knowledge and ideas which make thought possible. A crucial question concerns the depth and range of study which will be required in order to achieve the state of autonomy. It is possible to acquire superficial knowledge which enables a student to understand and perhaps repeat other people's arguments and propositions but without being able to use the ideas and facts in fresh and imaginative ways. This is not true autonomy and here lies one of the dilemmas. In order to achieve autonomous thinking considerable specialization may be necessary and the autonomy is possible over a small range of knowledge only. This might not be regarded as wide enough to count as a liberal education and although higher education is sometimes equated with liberal education, higher education can be narrowing. The final problem therefore is whether liberalization and specialization are incompatible notions and whether a broad education designed to have mass appeal is either sufficiently liberating or a 'higher' education.

References

PEDLEY, R. (1977) *Towards the Comprehensive University* Macmillan.
WARNOCK, Mary (1977) *Schools of Thought* Faber & Faber Ch. 11.

2. Higher Education for All in Today's Society

Geoffrey D. Sims

In chapter three the academic implications of higher education will be discussed from a primarily philosophical viewpoint. By contrast this chapter will concern itself more with what exists and the extent to which it is serving both the needs of the individual and of the public at large who indirectly pay for it. This is not to say that philosophical considerations can ever be absent from a proper consideration of the subject – but given that our present system is not 'ideal' we need to examine it with a view to seeing whether it can fulfil the broader functions in the future, which universal higher education implies. Let us then first consider the likely attitude of the public insofar as we can divine it.

Asked whether they considered education to be a good thing, most people would reply instantly 'Yes, of course it is', but the extent to which they regard higher education as desirable, is a less certain matter. Some societies, such as those in North America, have regarded it as natural for an extremely high proportion of their population to receive extended education, whilst in Europe things have moved very much more slowly. Even in Europe however, attitudes differ, for although the proportion of the appropriate age group receiving higher education (1·1 to 1·5 per cent) does not vary widely between countries, the esteem accorded to the recipients does. In the United Kingdom, following the post-Robbins euphoria, the government has shown rather less enthusiasm for further developments in higher education than would have been expected a decade ago. In this chapter I shall endeavour to discuss some of the reasons for this situation and, at the same time, try to suggest what our attitudes to the future should be. In doing this I do not wish to confine my remarks entirely to the United Kingdom for it is extremely helpful to contrast the approaches being used in different parts of the developing world as well as in other nations in Europe and America. First however let us examine the present institutions of higher education which are at our disposal.

Academic higher education in the United Kingdom

Traditionally the universities have been the vehicles for higher education in the United Kingdom. At the start they were ecclesiastical foundations functioning primarily as centres of learning and learning alone. By the mid-nineteenth century there was much debate about what the true nature of a university should be. Newman and others argued strongly that it was far from clear that teaching and research needed to co-exist in the same institution. Systematic research was, at that time, in many respects under-developed although there were at last beginning to be signs in the sciences of a more rational approach to scholarship. For the rest there was consider-able intellectual debate, some of which resulted in true scholarship while much of the remainder could be dismissed as attempts on the part of individual scholars or groups to influence others towards their views.

After the Second World War the universities had not only multiplied in number but also in kind and more were to come. We had, on the one hand, the great medieval institutions of Oxford and Cambridge. Alongside them stood the later developed but similarly traditional foundations, which included the Scottish universities, whilst the University of London with its enormous network of colleges preparing people for external degrees was unique. The great civic universities, most of which were founded around the beginning of the century, represented scholarship of a high class, albeit in a red-brick setting. Later, there would come the 'new' universities, determined to find original approaches to learning and the, in some ways ill-fated, Colleges of Advanced Technology, soon to become universities themselves, which had originally been founded to meet those rather specific needs of industry which were not, at that time, thought to be provided for by the universities.

The one thing that all these institutions held in common was that now they accepted that the advancement of knowledge (research) and teaching must go hand in hand. It was necessary to be actively engaged in research in order to earn your right to teach. The demand for more higher education had already started to produce its problems. In the fifties the universities were seen as ivory towers with little connection with the outside world and although many had strongly developed extra-mural departments, they tended to be treated by the universities as appendages with not very much relevance to mainstream activities. It was this situation of isolation and rigidity which challenged the new universities to develop differently and which encouraged an exasperated industry to accept from government the idea of the ephemeral Colleges of Advanced Technology which were soon themselves clamouring for full university status. Yet in practice, the new universities were not so different from the old although their groupings of studies tended to be more inter-disciplinary, so that one found the emergence of Schools of European Studies, of Latin-American Studies and of Applied Sciences rather than some of the more restrictive 'vertical' headings to be found in most university calendars.

By the late sixties we had a substantial university provision which was starting to evolve in response to the expressed needs of society. Indeed it was not long before certain faculties, at least in the older established universities, had already turned their attention quite strongly in this direction. Signs of this were seen in the direct involvement of engineering faculties with industry, a concern with 'applicable' science, a recognition of the role of applicable social science and indeed, in many quarters, a belief that a subject which was 'vocational' had a proper place within the university framework and was not something to be denigrated as a second-rate field of study.

Nevertheless, the nation's industry was not entirely satisfied, although many argued that industry did not know what it wanted and indeed could never 'express its needs' because their very diversity is such that no succinct statement is possible. There was however an undoubted demand for more people to be produced through the higher educational process, who were industry-directed, than the universities were seen to be developing at that time. The Robbins Report (HMSO 1963) had given us the prospect of graduates in abundance, but would their education be 'relevant'?

Suddenly the 'binary system', which resulted in the creation of some thirty polytechnics, was with us. The polytechnics were to prepare people for degrees just as the universities did, while at the same time they would cater for other levels of training to include the higher national diplomas appropriate to technician qualification in industry. This function had previously been almost exclusively the preserve of the colleges of further education, but there was clearly much sense in blending the technican engineer function with that of the education of the professional engineer under one roof. The polytechnics were not intended to be research-oriented and their main aim was to produce the 'useful people that industry needed'.

Time was to prove that this was far too naive an approach to the solution of the problem. First, it was to take many polytechnic institutions a long time to build up the necessary staff competence and facilities to do the job which had been given them. Secondly, many of their staff felt that they too wished to undertake research for much the same reasons that a university teacher would, while thirdly, and perhaps most importantly, the poly-technics had to face the very great difficulty that the universities were there already and for a long time were to continue to attract the best students in terms of academic ability. Faced with a student shortage the polytechnics began to diversify their coverage and far from merely directing their efforts towards manufacturing industry, which had been the primary need, they became much broader institutions than had been the original intention. Certainly it was intended that they should cover many of the areas which universities did not touch to any great extent at that time, but the emergence of substantial schools of philosophy, for example, had not been a part of the original polytechnic conception. Today, whilst fulfilling the expectations of their founders very successfully, in certain areas of endeavour, it is surprising to find that the proportion of arts-based students is, on average, currently of the same order as that in the universities themselves.

In addition to the universities and polytechnics there continued to exist the large distribution of teacher training colleges which single-mindedly pursued their defined task of producing teachers for primary and secondary education to meet the needs of a nation whose birthrate had risen rapidly following the end of the Second World War. In certain respects their approach had also changed for an increased professionalism within teaching generally saw basic teacher training courses extended from two to three years thus putting them on a footing with the other institutions where courses of a minimum of three years in length were the norm. The majority of colleges functioned under the wing of the universities, through area training organizations who ensured that appropriate standards were met and were responsible for seeing that teachers were given some degree of in-service training. In the late sixties Bachelor of Education degrees, validated by the universities, started to appear in the colleges and these proved to be both attractive to students and successful in producing a more thoroughly educated and trained teacher than the colleges had been able to manage hitherto. All was going well until the sudden realisation in the first half of the seventies that the birthrate, far from continuing to increase, was plunging rapidly and the numbers of teachers in training needed to be drastically reduced. With this realisation came the report of the James Committee (HMSO, 1972) which sought not only to look into the future qualifications of teachers but to try to see a new role for the teacher training colleges which might, in the near future, be able to play a broader role in higher education. The James' recommendation for a new qualification, the Diploma of Higher Education, met with a lukewarm response, though it had the effect on many of the colleges of causing them to think about their future in much less restrictive terms. Some colleges wished not only to initiate Dip.H.E. courses but, encouraged by the success of the B.Ed., to go still further by initiating their own degree courses to be validated by the universities or by the CNAA. In the event however a crisis occurred in 1976 and far from there being a substantial extension of higher education facilities along 'Liberal Arts College' lines a great number of the teacher training colleges were closed down whilst the majority of the rest were either merged with polytechnics or put under their aegis rather than that of the universities.

I have dwelt on this last period, not so much for its importance to teacher training *per se* but because it provides a very sharp and interesting example of the problems to be confronted in the design of any higher education system. Clearly we were not effectively planning our teacher training production programme with a view to real need – a criticism valid for almost all other areas where needs for specific categories of trained personnel can be identified. At the same time we were also facing the results of extreme national economic difficulty, though the opportunity to expand the numbers of people going into higher educational institutions was there, for the existing colleges and their staffs were available and in some cases keen to accept a new kind of student. In this context it is entirely proper to ask if the students would wish to come to these institutions, had they survived as Liberal Arts Colleges, offering a Diploma of Higher Education which in itself was not job-oriented. It is quite clear that in other countries the answer would have been yes, but much depends on the value that society puts on higher education for its own sake. Perhaps they would in the UK too, but for the time being we shall not know because closure or submergence of the colleges was the chosen solution rather than a determined attempt to try the experiment: economic difficulties alone determined the course of events.

In this example therefore we see in relief three of the major factors likely to fashion the shape and future of any system of higher education, viz: *student preference*, *manpower planning*, and *what society can afford*. All of these aspects need to be thought about very seriously and are discussed either in later parts of this chapter or elsewhere.

It is only in passing that we have mentioned the extra-mural departments which were initiated as sources for the extension of liberal education. They remain today financed by the DES for this same non-vocational purpose and are thus severely constrained in their ability to develop post-experience work on a broader canvas – an area again in which there seems to be a great need and an evident lack of overall policy. For many years we awaited the publication of the Russell Report (HMSO 1973) on adult education for it was abundantly clear that there was a need for the adult population to continue its studies, whether for recreational or professional purposes, later into life. When the report appeared in 1973 its recommendations were welcomed but once again we were not ready, economically, to grasp the nettle and so for the time being extra-mural departments still have to mark time whilst awaiting some encouragement to go forward on a grander scale with the task that unquestionably needs to be done.

Part One: The Academic Implications

It is interesting to reflect that the Cambridge University extension movement of the mid-nineteenth century (see, for example, Chapman 1955) provided the stimulus for the foundation of some of the great northern universities. There is equally a need for the university extension courses today and it is entirely proper that the polytechnics should continue to play their part in this area too.

In 1969 a further dimension was added with the foundation of the Open University which provided what were essentially home study courses for degrees making the maximum use of broadcasting as a teaching adjunct. Its creation clearly satisfied an unspoken need for housewives, craftsmen, people in retirement and a host of others, all of whom flocked to accept the intellectual challenge of higher education through the medium of 'distance learning'. The Open University, in its turn, showed just what could be achieved with really well-prepared written course material and an extensive and well organized network of tutors nationally available to its students. Although there may well be something in the argument that the initial success of the OU was due to a large pool of able but hitherto frustrated people wanting to achieve degrees, it seems likely that though the pool may be lowered it will never be completely drained. Although the demand for its services as a degree-awarding body may become less, there will inevitably remain an increasing role for the OU as a provider of post-experience courses. The Open University has given an object lesson to other institutions of higher education in how to communicate and any consideration of universal higher education in the future must accept the academic implications of its work.

There will be many who argue that nothing can beat the personal tutor/student relationship on which the modified Socratic method of the older universities was founded. Equally many will argue that this approach cannot be applied to the immense numbers of people for whom the higher educational system will have to cater in years to come. There is no doubt that we must reappraise not only our needs, but the ways in which we seek to satisfy them and this implies the need for some radical changes in the attitudes of teachers in higher education.

Reading the above summary of the position of higher educational institutions in the country today the reader may be forgiven for concluding that Britain is just muddling through. Given that any system of universal higher education, however well planned, must always be in a state of change, particularly when so many new aids to communication continue to become available to us, it might be more generous to comment that what we have at the moment is 'an interesting plurality', which can and must evolve in time into the ideal, for which we all sense the need but which has yet to be well defined. Whatever our deficiencies we have certainly retained a high degree of autonomy and academic freedom in the universities which is the envy of many, and whatever other shortcomings may be evidenced, high-quality graduates continue to be produced at lower costs than in most other developed countries.

The attitudes and needs of technological society

We have commented on the idealism of the traditional university, although, as we have hinted already, the old 'ivory tower' attitude no longer commands the deference of a society which is more concerned with its own material needs. Lest this should sound like an implied moral judgement I hasten to make the point that not all materialism should be considered as bad, for a manufacturing country like the United Kingdom must develop its capacity to produce goods and to sell them abroad in order to provide the resources to sustain any higher educational system at all. There is thus a certain 'chicken and egg' situation here, in that industry needs to be fed by the output of an appropriately directed higher educational system before it can produce the resources with which to maintain it. This need in itself has academic implications in that it is not necessarily compatible with a universal application of, for example, the Robbins Report principle of 1963.

What then is the future of the ivory tower? The health of any society depends upon the preservation of its culture as well as its long-term economy and this in turn dictates the need for scholarship in the traditional mould. It is balancing this need against that for vocationally-trained personnel to sustain the wealth-producing process which constitutes the major problem of today: a problem which faces all societies to varying degrees, whatever their state of development.

In the areas of science and technology particularly there was, for a long time, the belief that *all* research was potentially useful to industry. Enormous sums of money were spent with this thought in mind, but in today's harder society the question is being asked with increasing frequency 'to what extent will this piece of work really be useful in helping us to do this or that better?' Of course the answer can never be given with certainty. Some of the greatest, and most industrially valuable, discoveries have emerged from pieces of work which were not in any way directed towards that end. Equally, much scientific enquiry, although of great academic interest, is highly unlikely to do anything more than elucidate the detailed nature of processes which we are already able to use. It is therefore arguable whether 'much of the pure research in the natural sciences has been *done*' and that future investigation should be regarded in the same way as research in the humanities, and budgetted for accordingly as a contribution to our cultural rather than to our material advancement. Since national needs fluctuate, so too will society's support for such research activities. This simple polarization, however, into 'desirable but irrelevant' subjects and 'relevant' subjects is a gross over-simplification of our situation and one which is all too often made. It is nonetheless a useful starting point for a discussion.

The United Kingdom has, for centuries, encouraged amateurism. The foundation of our Civil Service and our Diplomatic Service has fostered the cult of the amateur and indeed the argument for its having done so is a powerful one. To recruit people for their innate ability, rather than for their expertise, may often be a better policy than to recruit someone who is second-rate, but whose education is apparently directed towards serving an immediate end. Provided that the education which an individual has received has given him a sharp, flexible mind, it is arguable that he should be able to turn himself to any path and this has been the foundation of much public service provision in this country for several centuries. But the time has come when many affairs of vital importance to the nation need contributions from those with special expertise, often of a vocational nature. The upholders of traditional education in the humanities often hold views biased by their own success, a success which was achieved in the absence of any real competition from other disciplines and in times which are no longer with us, so rapid has been the change over the last two or three decades. There is clearly always a need for people who, because of their lack of detailed professional grasp can look at situations dispassionately. The professional is always apt to get too involved with the detail because he understands the problem too well. It is important however that we should not take this argument too far – for in today's society it can be a positively dangerous one!

We are now firmly in the age of the professional: his skills have been developed at university or polytechnic on a full-time basis and will, in due course, be directed into employment which draws heavily on those professional skills. In many areas of employment particularly in the 'high technology' industries, the relevant knowledge today will become totally irrelevant tomorrow and as I have already intimated the provision of adequate post-experience education becomes essential merely to keep up to date with the needs of the time. Here we face another dilemma, for the nation has been slow to respond to the creation of an adequate system of post-experience education. The logical solution to the problem is that the first degree course should concentrate heavily on 'fundamentals' and leave the more ephemeral vocational aspects to be dealt with by 'experience' or subsequent short-course education. But this system tends to produce instruments which industry is presently slow to sharpen. The result has been that, in many cases, our institutions of higher education have tended to fall rather between two stools by producing the man with applicable knowledge at the expense of the development of his longer-term critical faculties. This criticism strikes at the very philosophy which underlies the establishment of the polytechnics, though it must be accepted that many polytechnics have realized the difficulties they face in this area and have not succumbed to temptation.

Whatever the truth of the above analysis we have not so far referred to the needs and aspirations of the individual. Young people form their ideas about what they want to do (or more often about what they do *not* want to do) as a result of combinations or pressures involving parents and teachers, what they read in the newspapers about likely job prospects, and on the basis of information drawn from a variety of arbitrary sources, many of which are of doubtful accuracy. For the parent and the teacher academic success still tends to be something which is seen as being a primary target for those in their charge and the need to pursue a recognized qualification is held up as paramount. Perhaps the greatest limitation to this process is that it is not always apparent that the perceptions of those involved extend far beyond their own fields of study or experience. The Robbins Report criterion, therefore, which advocated the universal provision of places in higher education for suitably qualified young people to study subjects of their own choice is a reflection and indeed a consolidation of this difficulty.

It is plain that a young person studying a subject towards which he is strongly motivated is more likely to succeed than someone directed into a course that he doesn't really want to do and I would not for one moment wish to argue against this truism. The quality of advice available, however, is often indisputably extremely poor and a very high proportion of young people enter into higher education without ever having considered the full spectrum of possibilities which might have been open to them. At present many young people are more likely to be primarily motivated by their perceived career prospects than by their superficially strongest academic skills and there is thus often a tension between what is expected of them by their elders and what they see as being rewarding in the future, albeit on the basis of often dubious understanding on both sides. The almost total freedom which underlies our approach to higher education in this country is something to be prized, but unless we can find a better way of reconciling the manifold needs of our society with the higher educational process, this very freedom in the end may become self-destroying because it presently appears to command neither the respect of the government nor of the *vox populi*.

It is interesting to contrast our approach to that used in developing countries. In some ways those developing countries which started their university institutions first were at the greatest disadvantage because, in many cases, their universities tended to be carbon copies of our own institutions and far from meeting the immediate needs of their societies they produced people more fitted to a Western pattern which had little in common with the cultural or material needs of, for example, a tropical or a desert region. Those that started later have tended to see their universities very much more as instruments of national need and many have been created more in the mould of our own polytechnics. This parallelism was certainly not, in most cases, a conscious decision to imitate on their part. It sprang more from a realistic appraisal of what was most needed at their particular stage of development. This all makes good sense and there are many splendid examples of countries which recognize the need to contribute both to the propagation of their culture and to the more materialistic calls of development.

The developing world, however, has inevitably, in the first instance, been dependent on aid from more developed countries and this in itself has not always been as effectively directed as it could be. To a Western mind it often seems natural that the best way of helping a developing country is to make a contribution to 'rural development' and many Western nations have concentrated their aid policy in this direction. The recipient countries often properly argue that rural development is not necessarily the best way forward, in that if you have a starving population you may very well meet its needs more appropriately by building battery chicken houses in your cities rather than by trying to cope with a recalcitrant soil in an inhospitable climate. What has obviously been lacking has been a proper dialogue between the consumers and the suppliers of aid in defining the purpose of the education. Developing countries need teachers of physics and of languages every bit as much as developed countries do and aid programmes need to recognize this. A particular reason however for introducing the problems of the developing countries at this point is that in a strange sense they resemble our own on the issue of 'relevance'. To produce people through higher education whose needs are 'relevant' requires a dialogue between the consumer, the provider of the money and the provider of the education and all too often this does not take place in an effective and meaningful way. It also requires a kind of wisdom in relation to the 'value' of an education which is usually not clearly in evidence. We shall discuss the role and virtues of 'relevant' institutions later on, but first we shall consider how these problems and attitudes exert pressures upon the educational institutions and their members.

Society's pressure on the 'Academics'

Although the discussion which follows is couched very much in the context of today it is illustrative of a much wider situation since many of the problems are of a recurring nature and will have to be faced from time to time anywhere where the 'universalization' of higher education proceeds.

If one merely attempts to meet the needs of a changing society by propagating more and more of the same types of institution, costs will increase roughly in proportion to the additional numbers of students admitted. The United Kingdom is not the only country to have reached the point where the cost of the higher educational system is felt to be prohibitively large. It is not surprising that government should call for 'unit costs' to be reduced, yet over-application of this pressure is incompatible both with the preservation of the essential character of the institutions concerned and with a maintenance of worthwhile academic standards.

In universities the effects of cost reduction manifest themselves in two basic ways. First, there is a natural inclination, though strongly resisted by the academics, for staff/student ratios to deteriorate, with the apparent consequence that the quality of education must fall. Secondly, with less money available, there is less support for research work and, because of increased teaching responsibilities, less time for it as well. This suggests that the effective 'quality' of the members of staff as teachers will fall also. It is true that with an intelligent reappraisal of how best to teach one's subject something can be done with modern technological aids to offset the apparent falling standards of teaching, but in research there is little room for compromise because either you do your research in a proper, scholarly, rigorous way, or it is not worth doing at all. Today's university staff are therefore faced with a dilemma which does cause considerable distress. Many, recruited in the Robbins period, experienced a heyday in terms of what it was possible to do within the university context, where money imposed little constraint and where, because career prospects and morale were high, any problems which did exist were faced with optimism and could be surmounted. It is now difficult for them not to regard that period as defining 'normality'. In fact it was not in any sense normal and the difficulty of returning to a more temperate level is very great for everyone concerned particularly since the planned expansions were never carried to completion and many institutions were left in a stressed off-balance condition.

The pressure is felt most of all perhaps when the universities are called upon to become yet more outgoing institutions and to play an ever increasing part in post-experience education, contributing to spheres of activity which today's staff do not see as traditional work of the university teacher. The size of the problem varies very much according to discipline. The teacher in the humanities is clearly upset when he cannot achieve the same close tutorial relationship to which he has been used, whilst the teacher in pure science is probably more concerned with his ability to maintain what he sees as an adequate level of research. Clearly in making such a generalization one is assuming that both sectors are equally hard-pressed in terms of the numbers of students that they have to teach. This assumption is not currently true across the whole field of science and in some areas, as a result of the falling off in the interest of students, staff/student ratios remain extremely favourable and there is a tendency to resent those departments whose ability to get on with their research, and therefore apparently enhance their career prospects, is unhampered by an excessive teaching load.

In other disciplines different attitudes persist. Law faculties, for example, customarily seem to work with quite poor staff/student ratios without showing signs of undue strain. Relationships with the profession that they serve, on the whole, seem to be good and it is not greatly held against the 'academics' that many of the teachers in Law departments have never practised. In engineering, on the other hand, staff/student ratios usually also tend to be quite high and the engineers, most of whom have practised, are acutely conscious of the need to keep active contact with their profession. This imposes an additional burden, but there is a manifest willingness to undertake, for example, short-course work, both inside and outside the university and this is an accepted part of the commitment even though the pressures which it generates are extremely high. We are therefore in a situation where most academics are under stress either because of real situations which make greater demands upon their time than it is reasonable to expect, or because the nature of their job commitment and expectation has changed and they are no longer facing the same job prospects and demands that they had come to expect when they were recruited. Some are more willing to adapt than others but willingness alone is not always enough, for in many cases the pressures are such that people cannot reasonably be expected to do any more.

Similar situations pertain in many developing countries where universities originally set up primarily as teaching institutions are being found to take a far higher proportion of the nation's total educational budget than was foreseen. They are therefore pressed to give more service, through self-help, participation in rural development, distance learning schemes and the provision of a multiplicity of community services ranging from land survey and collection of population statistics to widespread medical care. The underlying philosophy in these situations is often rather different in that, in many cases, the universities represent the greatest concentration of expertise in their countries. It is therefore natural to expect such help but, even if finance was sufficient, adequate manpower is seldom available for, in a world where instant communication has made everyone aware of what can be done, desires often move ahead at a faster pace than the ability to fulfil them.

The academic in a university in a developing country may well therefore have more expected of him, than in a developed situation, and with fewer resources of any kind at his command. Furthermore, such universities often tend to be far more the creatures of government than in the UK and the tensions between the need to be politically acceptable and to exercise reasonable academic freedom can become extreme.

It may be asked what relevance the description of these present problems, particularly those in the UK, has to the future of universal higher education. I have dwelt on it for several reasons. The first is to illustrate the fact that one cannot just talk of a university, for different disciplines have different attitudes which affect the whole area of universal higher education. Some disciplines recruit naturally outgoing and flexible people: others, because of the academic tradition which has been formed over the centuries, do not, belonging to a world where the freedom of the academic to develop his scholarship unhampered by outside constraint has been regarded as a fundamental for a very long time. There is an inevitable reaction when that freedom appears in any way to be limited. From the point of view of society, it is absolutely essential that academic freedom interpreted in the proper sense should be maintained, for universities should never become mere tools of government or any other political faction. It must always be their role to pursue scholarship dispassionately but there is no reason at all why this role should not be compatible, at least in part, with the material needs of society. Every institution therefore has its own kind of pluralism and should be able to practise and justify it.

The second reason is to show the difficulties which institutions founded in one age face in adapting to another, particularly, in respect of vocational demands. Staff appointed for life get 'set in their ways', yet there are strong arguments for a substantial degree of permanence if research work and true deep scholarship is to flourish.

The polytechnics, as they have been evolved, have had to face a rather different kind of task. Being of rather more recent origin, with more clearly defined aims, they have been able to structure themselves to approach their present specified objectives more easily. Time will show to what extent they too can serve as flexible and adaptable instruments working to meet the mistily perceived needs of the society of the day. The polytechnics' problems in the future may well manifest themselves more strongly in those areas where in times of student shortage they have expanded (for example in the humanities) but where they were never originally intended to deploy a substantial part of their effort. The difficulty of their task will be exacerbated by their having had to absorb many of the teacher training colleges for not all of the staff acquired in this process are necessarily oriented towards the original basic purposes of the polytechnics.

Considering universities and polytechnics together then, we see an interesting contrast and yet some remarkably common problems. The universities of the post-Robbins era were expected to respond to a student demand in all disciplines whilst the polytechnics were primarily intended to fulfill an industrial need. The pressures of society have forced upon the universities the responsibility of also responding to the needs of both industry and commerce, whilst the polytechnics, through student shortage, have expanded into other areas giving them a coverage which is in many cases not dissimilar from that of the universities. The common problem is how flexibility can be achieved in the face of a future which we know can change extremely rapidly indeed. It is possible that if we were to plan our 'ideal' educational system we would not want to start from where we are at the moment – but that is perhaps a speculation which we should not dwell on at this point!

Before leaving the subject of pressures on the institutions and the academics themselves it would be appropriate to refer again to the difficulties of contributing to post-experience education in a country which accepts the need for it but is reluctant to provide resources. Rapid changes in technology, rapid changes in legislation and rapid changes in professional practice, all help to sustain this need, not only in industry but in public bodies such as the health service and local government. In some such sectors there is limited ability to pay for post-experience education for many categories of staff whilst others can readily receive it in greater measure. It is, further, far from clear that the greatest need and the ability to pay are in any way correlated. In industry, fed generously by graduates from a state-sponsored educational system, there is a general and remarkable reluctance to spend very much money or the further education of its professional men who, it often argues, cannot be spared from important wealth-creating work merely in order to indulge in more education. The management area is perhaps an exception but industry cannot live by managers alone! The problem must, sooner or later, be tackled, and however powerful the role of the Open University model may prove to be, it cannot solve the problem on its own.

It is interesting also to note how different national legislative policies can affect this situation. For example, the first industrial training act in this country (1968), which required firms to pay levies to training boards for the purpose of staff education, resulted in a reaction which contributed greatly to the development of the abilities of craftsmen and of technician grades in industry. This was a wholly desirable turn of events but the fact that the Act also allowed the money so collected to be used for the education of graduate staff was largely disregarded and this resulted in very little being accomplished. By contrast in France (1971), similar legislation brought in somewhat later concentrated on *education permanente* aimed almost exclusively at graduate-level personnel. The numbers of short courses run in the Paris Grandes Ecoles alone and the numbers of students attending them makes a sorry contrast with the total, yet microscopic, efforts made in this country.

Where next?

It is clear that many factors have to be balanced one against another if we are seeking to define any kind of ideal. The concept of the 'whole man', in educational terms, is an extremely attractive one but the fact remains that many people who seek to enter higher education today are not particularly interested in becoming 'whole men'. Furthermore, at a time when we need people with vocational higher education the task of producing rounded, educated men in the classical mould, who also have professional skills, is not only an expensive and lengthy process but would not usually be acceptable to the young man wanting to prepare himself as quickly as possible to earn a salary and to settle to married life.

Our ideal solution must depend on the reconciliation of what individuals want and what society needs and this in turn depends very much on the *values* of the society of the day. It is beyond question that we must afford sufficient education but what is sufficient?

Nationally we need 'whole men', we need well-educated professionals, we need people who will contribute to our culture, we need people who will create wealth. None of these needs are mutually exclusive but the degree to which they can be met in any one person is very much a function of the individual and of his abilities and motivations. Any higher educational system which seeks to serve the nation and preserve its integrity in relation to its educational ideals must have a clear perception of its own role.

One of today's problems is that this clear perception is not there. Our educational system seems to be founded principally on the assumption that to study is good and that three years of higher education is the right amount for all but those entering certain professions. As a result of this process most of our institutions, whatever their official description, suffer from a certain confusion of identity although there is in principle no reason at all why the educated man, defined in classical terms, and the professional/ vocationally oriented man should not be produced in the same institution. One could argue this in other terms but there are undoubted benefits to be obtained from making the classically educated man practically aware and also from making the practical man culturally sensitive.

There are perhaps areas, for example within certain specialized branches of engineering where 'relevant' institutions clearly have their place. The 'relevant' institution, at undergraduate level, can however be an extremely dangerous concept if it merely serves to limit the horizons of the individual concerned. There is therefore a strong case for seeing relevant institutions as having a primary function at a postgraduate level and here the German academic institute provides an excellent model of how a specialized in- dustrial need can be integrated with a sound educational approach. This requires a joint participation of the industrial employer with those who seek to educate and research, in designing what the institute itself should attempt to do. It would seem preferable then, rather than to unduly bias our university education by trying to put quarts into pint pots at under- graduate level, to establish more institutes of this kind functioning on an independent basis, but at the same time closely associated with the univer- sities. At present there seems little real enthusiasm for sponsoring such developments, though the proven success of this approach in many countries around the world makes the strongest possible case for our following suit. I am inclined to argue therefore against the purely 'ivory tower' institution, and there are dual reasons for this view. First, many of the classical disci- plines today require the skills and techniques of the scientist to further their development while, secondly, to divorce disciplines in specialized institutions is the greatest enemy of cross-fertilization.

If we persist with basically mixed institutions resembling, for example, our traditional civic universities, what should be their proper range of functions? The following perhaps provides a basis:

1. They will have to provide a basic higher education for the school leaver, the nature of which will be somewhere between the ends of the spectrum defined by the traditional humanities on the one hand and more strongly vocationally-inclined courses on the other. There will be less difference in objectives between these courses than is often assumed, for any true university course must primarily be aimed at developing critical abilities, sensitivity, and the ability and desire in the individual to continue

to educate himself once he has left the university.

2. The courses offered will still need to lead to recognized qualifications, for despite the arguments against formal qualifications they are not only essential for the professions (who would wish to be operated upon by an unqualified surgeon?), but they provide a useful means of producing motivation among students. Where there is not some specific target to aim at this is often a real problem which should not be underestimated, particularly if we are talking in terms of truly universal higher education.

3. The lengths of courses need to be critically examined to ensure that the objectives can be realistically achieved within the time allowable. This could, in some cases, lead to degree course of less than two years while in others a four-year course will be more appropriate.

As we have already contended today's society will require an increasing provision of post-experience education and continuing education in other forms. Since, as we have argued, much of this is a proper function of the universities and polytechnics, it is essential that staff should be recruited who will recognize that this may be an important part of their duties. Once this recognition is there we shall have taken a large step towards a better provision for life-long education. It is important that programmes of this nature are developed in such a way as to use the full range of expertise available in all departments. In order to do this we need a critical examination of the continuing education organizations (e.g. extra-mural departments) in all institutions of higher learning, to ensure that they are integrated as fully as possible within the traditional life of the institution rather than being seen as something different and not really connected with the 'proper job' of a university teacher at all. In adding this responsibility to the normal range of work dealt with in universities it is essential to ensure that the staff concerned are not so burdened with teaching duties that they do not have the time to advance learning or to otherwise indulge in the professional practice essential to keep them in the forefront of their subject. Today's system fails because the post-experience element is usually something which people are asked to do as an extra when they are already fully committed to heavy teaching and research programmes.

As regards our more vocationally-oriented subjects, many of the professional institutions have failed lamentably either to guide the universities in regard to the needs of their professions or to encourage their practising members to take part in teaching such courses. The university institutions are not altogether blameless in this regard either and far closer collaboration in planning and execution of teaching programmes aimed at satisfying vocational needs is required than has been achieved in most cases up to the present. It is, however, the genuine desire of industry to provide the man hours to consider these problems and define their needs, which is often most lacking. For the rest the continuing education problem is immense whether one is aiming at the in-service training of school teachers or the mental satisfaction of geriatrics.

In summary then it may be argued that the universities and polytechnics, as institutions, should see themselves not just as places that prepare people for degrees but as places which involve themselves in the provision of education *for* life and *throughout* life. Clearly there are complementary roles to be played by further education colleges and other bodies, but the university tendency to cut off at the undergraduate or higher degree point will not suffice in the future. It is conceivable that the problem could be tackled by the provision of adult colleges, but both academic and economic reasons militate in favour of a better use of the universities which would benefit immensely from being seen as more open institutions. At present they are not perceived to be such; indeed in the minds of many, to enter the portals of a university building is to move into a world in which they feel, at best, insecure.

At the end of it all the greatest question outside the professional areas remains. What will the demand for universal higher education, either below or beyond degree level, turn out to be? When Sir Thomas More wrote *Utopia* he envisaged a society in which the hours of work would be relatively few because everyone pulled their weight and that in their extensive leisure time people would wish to educate themselves. He could not have foreseen that modern technology would have afforded a situation in which that time would be available to so many so soon, nor could he have envisaged the dense populations which exist in many countries. All of the signs, at the present time, are that although there is room for an enormous expansion in continuing education the attitudes of large sections of the public are not such as to conform to More's picture. I wonder to what extent this would remain true if we had really seriously attempted to tackle the problem?

References

CHAPMAN, A.W. (1955) *The Story of a Modern University* Oxford University Press, p. 13 *et seq.*

HMSO (1963) *Report of the Committee on Higher Education*, The Robbins Report, HMSO Cmnd. 2154.

HMSO (1972) *Teacher Education and Training*, The James Report, HMSO.

HMSO (1973) *Adult Education: a Plan for Development*, The Russell Report HMSO.

3. Education and the polity*

Bernard Crick

In times such as these some might think that it is their duty to defend unconditionally the sacred walls of education against the evil encroachments of politics. Freedom must, indeed, always be defended, but it can only be defended by politics. And spheres like 'education' and 'politics' are less easily distinguishable than most people imagine; definitions do not make or change social relationships; and empirically these two spheres are not autonomous, not even in principle.

So there follows not a rhetorical, public defence of the idea of education against the practices of politics, but rather a speculation about what education would be like if it followed political principles. To see education as responding to the political is something very different from seeing it reduced to the sociological. I may agree with the Marxists that all educational systems reflect and seek to perpetuate the values and customs of governing élites; but need not agree with them that all élites are based solely or even always primarily upon economic exploitation and class oppression. If I agree with them for the sake of argument that 'in the last analysis' the economic motive is dominant, yet I would still not agree that all élites are equally malign and would, indeed, modestly argue that some élites, by virtue of the ideologies or ideal images that they hold of human activity, are remarkably better than others. To say that education reflects the values of the political and social order is then, to my mind, a truism, something true for all societies, not a dramatic and specific unmasking of bourgeois-capitalist society. Whether on hearing such an utterance we shudder or nod, depends on what the values of the order in question are and on our own; and we cannot presume, except from the dogmatism of both Marx and Talcott Parsons, that these values are necessarily systematic and unified. A plurality of values is more often typical of human societies; and in human judgment, we have to weigh one value in conflict against another.

So, far from defending the idea of education against the practice of

* This is a revised and extended version of an inaugural lecture to the chair of Politics at Birkbeck College (University of London) delivered (very belatedly) on 20 January 1977, subsequently printed in the *Journal of Higher Education*, by kind permission of whose editors this appears.

coarse politics, I want to speculate about what the practices of education would be like if they followed the ideal of politics. We are used to economists treating education either as part of the economy or applying economic principles to its organization. Let us do the latter for political principles.

Such an enterprise will sound strange or shocking to the modern liberal, but would have seemed natural to the Greek and Roman republicans. What sort of education would we have, in other words, if we pursued more openly, honestly and consistently the idea of politics that we already possess in the Western tradition? Some of the Greeks had, after all, an ideal which, whatever happened to it in practice, however much negation of it, betrayal or falling short, has none the less dominated the imagination of the world ever since: the ideal of politics as being the public activities of free and equal men, the positive actions that constitute a state or polity composed of citizens. To be a free man was to have the right to participate and actually to participate, something quite unlike the modern liberal notion that liberty is being left alone from interference by the state.[1] And it is this negative liberalism that becomes advanced as if axiomatic, in every trite defence of academic freedom (by which people often seem to mean 'autonomy', which is impossible). As Hannah Arendt constantly argued, those who see civil liberties as withdrawal from politics should not be puzzled when they are then ignored and exploited by the state.[2] If this idea of making decisions politically (i.e. by citizens) seems trite, then contrast it to the more common ideas of leaving government to priests, warlords, technical experts, yogis or commissars, or in a word, to others.

The political tradition

The platitudinous, the obvious and the simple are often difficult to grasp. If we go badly wrong, we go wrong in our initial assumptions, less often in the technicalities of the entailments. So let me recall what the political tradition is about. Free-ranging speculation about what can be done through politics and the belief that man is at his best when active in a public arena, appears to be no older than the fifth-century Greeks. Plato was the first man whom we know drew a clear distinction between what is in fact *law* and what is in reason *just*, and then Plato went on to argue that men could construct either an ideal state (as in his dialogue, *The Republic*) or at least a very much better one, a rational compromise between the ideal and the real (as in his dialogue, *The Laws*). The contrast is vivid between the speculative Greeks, recognizing a variety of forms of government-and-society and believing that men could actually choose, if they fitted actions to words, which to have; and the otherwise almost universal acceptance in the ancient world of rulers and régimes as being an ordained part of divine order, or in the modern world, of objective necessity. But to Plato political freedom as creativity was to be limited only to those few who were capable of undergoing what one might call 'total education' culminating in a change of consciousness, the few shepherds of so very many sheep.

Aristotle first introduces wider, though still not complete, notions that human freedom is integral to justice and the business of good government. In his *Politics* he made three basic assertions – each of which I will apply as a critique of present educational arrangements.

First, he asserted that man is naturally a political animal. This embraces all that we might mean by saying that man is a social animal, but also something more: political man can act upon his environment in concert with his fellow men, not simply react. He can even create new cities and good laws. And he actually said that 'the man who can live outside the *polis* is either a beast or a god', for to be self-sufficient was not to be fully human. Perhaps he was thinking of his great pupil Alexander who, in breaking from the political relationship, could find no other title to claim to rule diverse cultures than that of being a god.

His second assertion is that society is composed of a diversity of elements. He says that his teacher Plato made the great mistake of thinking that a state without a single standard of righteousness is both unjust and unstable. Aristotle argues, on the contrary, against any attempt to apply a single standard, as tyrants and despots do. 'There is a point,' he says, 'at which a *polis* by advancing in unity, will cease to be a *polis*: there is another point, short of that, at which it may still remain a *polis*, but will none the less come near to losing its essence, and will thus be a worse *polis*. It is as if you were to turn [musical] harmony into mere unison, or to reduce a theme to a single beat.'

His third assertion is that 'mixed government' is the best, for he thought that a true polity was neither monarchy, aristocracy nor democracy alone (which he treated as pure types), but a creatives blending of elements. To call it a 'creative tension' would not be too far off, something between Plato's idea of dialectic as the method of philosophic argument and Hegel's idea of dialectic as the process of history. 'Democracy' to Aristotle is to be preferred to monarchy or aristocracy, if that is the only practical choice; but better than the rule of the *demos* alone (the mob, the poor and the ignorant) is a deliberate mixture of consent and power, the 'many electing the few', he says. His only possible justification of monarchy or rule by one man is, when that man is perfectly wise and perfectly good – a theoretical possibility, but since to the Greeks a perfectly good man would therefore become a god, the case is rather unlikely, as distinct from tyrants apeing gods. The only possible justification for aristocracy is wisdom and skill, but in practice the best, if put into office without rotation and the checks of democratic power, degenerate into an exploitative plutocracy, the rule of the rich. The only possible justification for democracy or rule of numbers is equality, but such a justification by itself is to Aristotle fallacious: 'the belief that because men are equal in some things, they are equal in all'. So it is better by far to tie the skill of the few to the need to get the consent of the majority, hence to controls by the majority; and if the few can carry the majority with them, then the state is far more powerful than a simple autocracy which keeps its people subdued. Much of Roman political thought and practice was just a footnote to this basic point: *'auctoritas in Senatum, potestas in populum'*—'always remember', as it were, 'that if skill and knowledge are in the Senate, power is with the common people'. And Machiavelli was to see, in this same tradition, that states that could make their inhabitants citizens, could then trust them with arms and thus find, with skill and civic patriotism combined, a power and a flexibility far greater than that of Princes, dependent as they were on cowed men or hired mercenaries. Gramsci was simply to see the skilled worker as the industrial equivalent of Machiavelli, Danton or Jefferson's citizen.

Moreover Aristotle argued that the fundamental way of changing a society from one type to another was through *paedeia* or education. Granted that with Aristotle, as Louis MacNeice remembered when he taught classics as humanism at Bedford College, 'But lastly we remember the slaves'. For Aristotle justified slavery as creating the leisure which was needed both for learning and for citizenship, so some see the very source of politics as tainted or as a proof that politics is only the subtlest method of class exploitation. But Aristotle also said that we will have slavery until we have the machines of Prometheus to work for us. As now we do. For the first time in human history there is the possibility of both political activity, educational attainment and welfare for all. It is our neglect of will and of reason if we do not make better use of the machines. We should no more blame the inherent structure of society than we should blame the stars themselves.

With the possibility of education for all, moreover, even Aristotle's caution about democracy can vanish: any distinction between polity (as mixed government) and democracy as the rule of numbers should wither away with universal free education. Aristotle's criterion for political justice could be applied to everyone, not just to an élite of citizens: 'ruling and being ruled in turn'. The distinction between polity and democracy would vanish so long as democracy itself operated in a political manner, recognizing and respecting differences of values, striving to enhance human freedom and human knowledge, not simply to create, in Tocqueville's heavy words, 'a tyranny of the majority'.

Three broad inferences

It is the sin of the academic to be so long in getting to the point. Now follow three broad inferences for what education would be like had it emerged from a tradition of political thinking rather than from a Christian-scholastic tradition of those who know condescending to preach the truth to those fit to be saved or fit to join the clerisy. And after that, some half-a-dozen specific inferences for contemporary policy are suggested.

1. From Aristotle's first concept that man is a political animal, it would follow very clearly that there should be more self-government at every level of education. In the government of schools and polytechnics and colleges of further education, the collegiate form of government should be the norm rather than both the ideal and the exception. In schools and polytechnics particularly the power of the head teacher or director in relation to his colleagues is one of the best anti-political examples for which any autocrat or bureaucrat could possibly wish. A school, for instance, may actually teach civics – if the head teacher wishes and if not, not. Even in universities and colleges of universities, one may loyally question whether such headships need be so permanent, whether they could not alternate, or power be far more rationally and functionally divided. After all, it is a Civil Servant and not a politician who is the permanent head of departments of governments; and he, if the politicians are worth their salt, carries out policy, not formulates it.

What complicates the call for more self-government in education, is that it is not clear what we should mean even by education as an institution. It would be ridiculously solipsistic and formal for us to think of colleges and schools as exhausting and monopolizing education. Are not books and libraries, newspapers, radio and television, and even the behaviour and speeches of public men part of education? And the family? We were in 1976–7 invited to debate the educational effect of schools and to discuss the proper role of parent, pupil and teacher participation in school government. But not, for instance, to have second thoughts about commercial advertising on television, which every teacher knows is among the most anti-educational practices of contemporary society. And we are not asked to consider how every type of educator should be involved: not just teachers, parents, politicians and officials, but journalists, librarians and publishers too. The debate proved rather narrow. For we do not live in isolated hutches.

Rather we live in a great big, interconnecting, and rather grubby, warm warren. 'Only connect', indeed.

2. From Aristotle's second concept that society is composed of a diversity of elements, it should follow that we should educate for diversity and not for consensus. Civilization 'as we know it' is not going to fall apart if schools do not teach good manners, good English, the tables, morals, docility and the British Constitution; rather it may be the case that even more alienation and resentment may occur among young people if schools try to carry the alarm clock back along such worn-out paths. An education for diversity would stress problems and critical method rather than offering authoritative solutions. And it would allow for the fact that freedom means acting spontaneously, not in some pre-determined manner; so that the student must be allowed time to ask the awkward and even irrelevant question, not simply the one that helps the orderly progression of a lesson (which could easily be built into a teaching machine). And it would let pupils and students make genuine choices at every age and at every level, both in cultural and vocational studies, only insisting that both are always present. The experience of choosing is a greater human value than memorizing blocks of assessable facts faster.

3. From Aristotle's third concept that the best form of government is mixed government, it would follow that much of the great debate about which parts of education shall be cultural, which vocational or productive and which 'political' or concerned with maintaining or changing the social system, that much of this debate is, in absolute terms, needless and meaningless. We need all three. Any society is necessarily involved in all three. If there is to be a common core, it must contain all three. But by looking at it politically, we might get the proportion better – as I will now try to do.

Policy implications

1 Timing

Hannah Arendt points out that political activity is something that must be carried out continuously.[3] In that respect it is rather like labour to earn food, fuel and clothing to stay alive: for most people there is little possibility of capital accumulation; so once we stop, the thing comes to an end. Whereas with a book or a work of art or a building, there is a sense in which it can be finished and yet remain, even if it can be forgotten or rediscovered or if its meaning or significance changes. I think that education is an activity in this sense. So it is odd, indeed, in a society wealthy enough (despite our present difficulties) to make choices, that we appear to have chosen to lump an incredible amount of education, most of it compulsory, in the first two decades of life: and then to let it all come to a stop. Well, not quite all, but expenditure on extra-mural, adult education and continuing education is very small indeed compared to that on secondary education. Indeed it is very small, I am bound to add, compared to university and polytechnic expenditure. If the budget is fixed, the resources should be spread far more widely through different kinds of institutions and throughout life.

At Birkbeck College, we have every right to blow our own trumpet, a little more boldly and loudly. We should not just say that we are offering the chance of a conventional university education to older people who missed out straight from school or who want to try again, to change course, or to refresh and refuel. We should say that we are doing something intrinsically better than the straight-from-school institutions. For many of the problems of the relationship of education to industry, many of the problems of pure as against applied, or culture as against technology, or of the intellectual as against the vocational, seem so much less pressing and so much more easy to resolve in practical ways when one is teaching and learning with people who have already been out and about in industrial society, in the world of work, post-experience rather than post-school. I don't say that evening part-time is always the best solution. Sandwich courses can work well. And there is room for a greater variety of experiment and experience in both, and indeed for more full-time study for mature students on the Coleg Harlech and Ruskin models; and for institutions of higher education to play a larger and a more responsible role in this, not just to offer cut-down segments of conventional single honours degrees. If we were able to stop and think, we might see that it does not help the values of a political civilization to pitch so many straight from school into three years of higher education. Even from the narrow self-interest of the traditionally academic university, it would help if they had grown up a bit or knew what they wanted. I have sympathy with the draconian views of the Swedish TUC who recently passed a resolution that no one should receive a university grant who had not first done two years of useful work in, or service for, society.

When the Robbins Report said that it was going to make a purely quantitative claim and was not concerned (ever so liberal) to say what should be taught, it in fact exhibited all that is worst in liberal economics: a pretence that large allocations of resources can be made without raising political and qualitative questions. When so many came up, we in the universities should have taught them differently, offered a much more deliberate mixture of intellectual and vocational subjects in a more general syllabus and abandoned the traditional single honours degree, at least until the taught or seminar MA level. Indeed, it was always an odd and self-interested argument to believe that a single honours degree, whether in Arts or in Engineering, was particularly likely to produce a well-rounded, cultured and effective person. We scholars should not have carried on so stubbornly and successfully creating students in our own image. Robbins' statistical proof that ever so many more could benefit from a traditional higher education than was once supposed, should have been seen as also proving that even more among less-favoured mortals could cope with lesser offerings, even shorter offerings of the same standard, at very different stages of life, not just in late adolescence or in the arrested adolescence that our famous new universities seem to have so successfully created in their youth-camp isolation.

To tell the truth, and to tell it at a nasty time as cuts rain down upon us, universities were over-expanded in the 1950s and 1960s. The university-educated élites acted recklessly and selfishly. They ignored adult, continuing and post-experience education, and the youth and community services, as being socially below the salt and economically irrelevant; and they left teacher training in proud but stagnant municipal isolation, instead of integrating it fully with higher education. Our rulers in peace exhibited, as Shaw remarked in the context of war, jobbery, snobbery and incompetence. Now I am not a sadist. I am not in favour of being cut about and bled at random as has tended to happen, but I do favour a massive re-allocation of resources within the whole education sector which university teachers would do well to join, not resist.

Political thinking, even on the humblest level, such as 'what sort of policies should the Labour Party have had?', would make one surprised that the London Birkbeck model, that is a full-time staff wholly devoted to mature and predominantly part-time students, was not applied to the other great conurbations; and that some of the misbegotten polytechnics, instead of copying conventional universities at supposed lower cost and with even more autocratic, bureaucratic government, should not have been turned – could not even now be turned – into Birkbeck-like institutions. The television access of the Open University has great virtues in open space, I mean for people trying to study outside the great centres of population. But the advantages of regular face-to-face teaching would seem obvious. Yet directed home-study has advantages and attractions to many; and certainly the innovations of the Open University in curricula construction have, by way of contrast, exposed the gentlemanly amateurism and the unreflective traditionalism with which so many university courses are strung together. If I claim that the Birkbeck model is, for the needs of most students, though not all students, a better one to follow than expanding the Open University, I certainly admit that Birkbeck has been all too conservative in curricular innovation, looking over its shoulders at the rest of London University, rather than considering the special needs of, and possibilities for teaching of and learning from, mature citizen-students.

Time press, otherwise a fairly obvious and by now well-known argument about time could be developed at the other end of the spectrum. Is it right or wise to keep fifteen and sixteen year olds full-time in school against their will, often with few visible results, except increased alienation (one does not need to be Ivan Illich to be a little worried here)? It is fairly natural for some people to want to work – in the ordinary sense of that word. Very few schools and very few firms work together to create any possibility of even part-time transition into industry or commerce. The dilemma would be less if governments had followed the logic of the Industrial Training Acts of the late 1940s and had extended – throughout all industry, commerce, administration and the professions – some spasmodic or even continuous day-release for education throughout working life.

2 Mobility

The political tradition in its ideal form, however bureaucratized some republics and political parties become in practice, encourages and thrives on mobility, adaptability, alternation of office, ruling and being ruled in turn. Universities however, long before some trade unions became nearly so powerful, have long established security of tenure for working life on criteria, which, once a person is appointed at all, are remarkably easy and routine to fulfil. In this they have followed in the footsteps of the great British Civil Service reforms of the 1850s and 1860s, establishing job security, incremental salaries and pensions. In the Civil Service this was done in the name of political neutrality. In the universities, it was done in the name of scholarship – or if signs of scholarship are utterly lacking, then it is said, *ipso facto*, that a man is a good teacher and his good teaching would be disturbed (will businessmen, lawyers and doctors please note?) by any occupational insecurity; not, as the economists would teach us, stimulated. Tenure too soon can mean ossification early.

What in fact happens is that very many people stay put in one place all their life, or at the best will make no more than one move. Take into account also the small size of the average department (a group who soon know each other's viewpoints inside-out, and are bored stiff with each other), and a stranger might be forgiven for thinking that a man would need almost superhuman powers of self-renewal not to lapse, by middle age, all too often into a pedantic and bureaucratic parody of his younger self. Is this good for teaching? Is this good for scholarship?

Are the abuses to which contracts shorter than life could give rise, greater or lesser than the risks of inertia? I am not sure, but the question needs raising urgently. Or if we insist on taking for granted the same occupational security as the pace-setters of the higher Civil Service (even if we as yet lack their inflation-proof and non-contributory pensions), could we resist a public and political demand that we should be treated as a Service and circulated from time to time, or perhaps not be promoted or allowed to pass the efficiency bar unless at least a third of our service had been elsewhere? If we want security, then mobility should be institutionalized. I can think of some stagnant pools called colleges where . . . no names, no pack-drill.

Consider that when tenure until sixty-five was given to the new Home Civil Service, life span was much as it is now, though life expectancy much less. Fewer people would have survived until sixty-five and, in any case, most higher Civil Servants or new university professors would have retired long before to look after the family property. Now we are all bureaucrats, hanging on to the last, few gentlemen. 'Sit on your arse for forty years and hang your hat on a pension', as Louis MacNeice sang.

Obviously I am raising a wider question about the fructifying effects of occupational mobility between education, administration, the professions and industry, not simply for individuals but for the economy. But I could linger on a narrower question simply for education. Should not ways be found by which we all teach in schools for a while, some also in further education, fewer in higher education; but none in one kind of institution for all their working life? And should not sabbatical entitlement be universal – why just in higher education? If it was compulsory and pension funded, it could apply to industry as well. Mobility should lead us towards versatility, which was a great cultural ideal in pre-industrial republics before division of labour became an ossified dogma rather than a partial necessity. And greater mobility would create much more mutual aid and understanding between education, government and industry. Politics involves mobility, then, which unavoidably involves some risk-taking and uncertainty: those who cannot live with this turn, in the modern world, to bureaucratic images of predictable, fully-pensioned order.

3 Space

The Greeks stressed that politics was a public activity and that a free-man does not live in isolation, he must emerge from the private shadows of the home and of the workshop into the public sunlight of the market place. And in terms of cultural and social history, both high culture and political and social reform are associated with great cities with assembly places, where different classes, creeds, functions, families, crafts and age-groups mingle and meet. Even the misogynist Thomas Hobbes says that: 'Leisure is the mother of Philosophy; and Commonwealth, the mother of Peace, and Leisure: where first were great and flourishing Cities, there was first the study of Philosophy'. And yet – am I passing from the sublime to the ridiculous? – we created at vast expense new universities with the names of famous cities, but all, without exception, as self-contained as possible and far outside the city walls! Why? Such uniformity argues a common cause. The obvious alternative would have been to have expanded the then quite small civic universities which were all, with two possible exceptions, firmly embedded in cities. Land values enter into it a little, but more important was an Oxbridge bias against industrial cities and industrial England exercised, moreover, by Civil Servants with the mentality of commuter-belt pseudo-gentry. Who can look at Kent, Warwick, Essex, Sussex, York and Lancaster without seeing the fagged-out end of the garden suburb movement? No wonder many of them have been such disturbed places. What collective lunacy or architectural arrogance ever thought of putting three thousand young people straight from school out in the fields together, as if learning and life can be divorced from the culture of cities, both high and low culture? In some ways these new buildings were worse than garden suburbs, for they represent an idea of a university as a refuge from the world of productivity, partly monastic in origins and partly arising from Matthew Arnold-like scorn for the common culture and for the new technologies that fed him and his pupils. Polity mixes groups, bureaucracy separates.

Citizenship – it is no empty truism – has much to do with living in cities; and so has a broad, not a narrowly liberal, education.

4 The Common Core: (a) knowledge

Skirmishing. Now to the hardest point. If we wish to preserve and extend political culture, a civilized one which is also productive, what kind of education should we have?

Bertrand de Jouvenal has well said that education has a dual purpose: 'to make man's labour more productive, and his leisure more fruitful. And the greater the gains in one direction, the more necessary is progress in the other'. But after saying that, he argued convincingly against any assumptions that education for efficiency and education for improvement are radically distinct, that 'to give both is twice as much trouble and takes twice as much time'. For he doubted that 'the time presently spent on education is well spent'.[4]

My political assumption is that education should serve industry quite as much as it serves learning and culture. But that our general educational institutions, like schools and colleges, will do this best not by training for specific jobs or by keeping up the cant that the liberally educated man can turn his mind and hands to anything – he plainly can't; but rather by defining an essential common core; by leaving plenty of time for choice of other subjects or part-time jobs; and by encouraging a greater versatility and practicality. Vocational and cultural education must not be rivals nor synthesized: they sit side by side, but should not merge and we should argue about the proportion of time in the timetable, not dominance of one over the other.

For the two main components of the common core, I will again follow De Jouvenal:

> Would anyone doubt that the art of correct expression (literature) and the art of rigorous reasoning (mathematics) are basic both to business and to culture? I would contend that the acquisition of these two skills is by far the most important part of education.[5]

These are the two forms of knowledge (and they are also transferable skills) which are essential, and from which everything else can follow. But everything else does not have to follow, all at once, certainly not in secondary school. So it would defeat the idea of a core curriculum if everything else that we have at the moment simply piled in afterwards. For room must be left for individual project work and crafts which, together with some education for political literacy, would constitute an education for practicality – so lacking in our formal culture at the moment. Let me notionally say that these three, literature, mathematics and practicality could each take a fifth of the time-table; then the remaining time must be a time for genuine options, an education in choice, and options must include the possibility of jobs: small jobs around the school for the youngest, part-time jobs in local shops, factories, offices or services and voluntary work for the older pupils. If deschooling would probably be disastrous, yet some relaxation of compulsion is needed when it so plainly does not work for the less-motivated and is not needed for the motivated.

Could the common core of knowledge be as small as literature and mathematics? Most of what we learn in school in 'history, geography, physics, chemistry, biology, or geology' (I shelter behind De Jouvenal again), is simply (i) forgotten as soon as it has been assessed and (ii) can be found in public libraries when wanted. He makes a massively simple point. What we need to know is where to find these things out in books and other sources of information when we need them and when we are interested. There is so much factual, purely-to-be-memorized lumber in the curriculum, only put there for assessment's own sweet sake. In most subjects in university, students could begin from scratch, indeed perhaps better than now, if a high standard of critical literacy and of numeracy was assured from the schools. 'My subject is, of course, different'; but unless it is English or mathematics, I doubt it. To dare to name names, history and geography are surely the greatest offenders in schools, remorselessly insatiable for yet another period and yet another area to be covered – remembered up to the exam and then forgotten. Whereas what historians and geographers say they want in higher studies is critical method. I hastily say that I am not arguing for no history or geography in schools (for most history is, in fact, treated exactly as if it were literature), but to have them and the others among the options, with tutor-teachers who concentrate on helping pupils to find out for themselves when and if they want to, in school or public library and elsewhere. And if they don't want to, so what? Will the pupils be less cultured, less effective, less decent as human beings? I cannot see the remotest reason why.

In other words, the political viewpoint would assume that we need both for nation-building and nation preservation, a minimum of national uniformity in the system; but beyond that, local diversity and personal freedom should flourish: both experiences are valid and needed.[6]

The political viewpoint would also support De Jouvenal in his basic contention that we do not need to choose between the scientific, the cultural and the vocational in the national, rational core. We must keep them separate. They each have their own logic and their own justifications. We should not try to produce thin, pretentious syntheses, but we should lay them each side by side both in curricula and in institutions. For as with the need for mobility, so much of the hopes for mutual understanding and respect between these different activities depend, not upon the formal curriculum at all, but on students of different areas rubbing shoulders in the corridors, canteens and common-rooms of polyglot institutions, where everyone must do a bit of each.

De Jouvenal, however, does not go quite far enough. True, he sees the need for a third leg to his stool – what he calls 'the art of checking factual statements', of weighing evidence, of finding alternative sources, a kind of education in practical scepticism.[7] I would agree and see this largely in terms of individual or small group project work, how to discover and check things in a critical spirit. But I would include in this practical information about welfare rights and employment and filling in forms, as well as intellectual discovery. Indeed many comprehensive schools do this kind of practical finding out very well already, calling it Social Studies, but in CSE for the least able; whereas the more able also need it, if they are to be practically minded. Indeed it is odd that the very successful 'play and discovery' methods of primary education are not applied to options throughout secondary and even higher education (sometimes a long research essay, occasionally projects). There is a good deal of evidence that formal learning and retention of it is actually enhanced by developing such skills. But I think that this third leg of De Jouvenal's needs extending more radically to be allied with political literacy and with crafts as part of a practical education.

The smallest component of this third leg, though an important one, is political literacy. It needs doing because politicians and the media provide so little on politics, economic and social problems that is genuinely educational. A little of it will go a long way, simply to teach and to discover together what the main issues and problems of contemporary society are thought to be, to examine different viewpoints on them in an empathetic way and above all, once again, to help pupils use alternative sources of information in a critical way. Much of political literacy can be acquired from the proper running (rarely as at present) of a school itself, above all observing the relationship of head teachers to their staff; but some knowledge of national and local issues is necessary. But I see this as a very simple thing, not needing the disciplines of politics, economics and sociology, all of which, to my mind, would have no place as such except as 'do-it-yourself' options in a school system reformed to correspond to the principles of polity.

Far more important for this third leg, however, (important in the sense of demanding far more time) is to remedy the neglect of basic practicalities. Things worth studying for their own sake must, indeed, be studied for their own sake, hence without compulsion, beginning with some instances at school and having the choice of all disciplines in higher and continuing education. But there cannot be, without great harm, a permanent divorce between culture and industry. The solution, however, is not to teach technology, or particular local trades in schools, but is to nurture a technological spirit and competence in practical ways.

5 The Common Core: (b) Practicality

By practicality I simply mean that an educated man should be able to tackle most of the small technical problems that he meets in everyday life.

Consider woodwork and handicraft. These are tiny gestures in that direction, usually compulsory only way down the school, often for the 'less able', usually skimped for the more academically able when faced with the over-loaded disciplinary timetable – that is skimped for those very people who may need it most, if one thinks of the technological illiteracy of our political and administrative élites. Practicality and technological awareness is not to be taught directly then, but may start with woodwork and metal work, progress to repairing bicycles, motor-bikes and routine servicing and minor repairs to cars; the repair of common domestic, electrical apparatus; painting and decorating, where arts and crafts and chemistry may be said to touch; the whole range of how to use well the new and culturally most interesting 'do-it-yourself shops'; how to record music and perhaps something about the music; repairing and making of clothes; cooking and knowledge of sources of dietetic and consumer information; and even typing. These should be as natural a part of the curriculum as physical and health education, and should be done irrespective of sex. Think of those ninnies in administration and universities who cannot even type a draft themselves – perhaps a memorandum on efficiency, written in longhand wasting the time of skilled secretaries, or think of proud beauty who cannot mend a fuse or inflate a tyre.

This all should be part of a common education for a new common man. The basic experience of making and repairing things is surely the first stage in making us all productivity-minded, without in any way impairing intellectuality and culture.[8] A person who cannot use his mind reflectively or creatively, who cannot use his hands and who cannot take action politically, this person should be thought of as less than a full and educated person – the Greeks would have said, not fit to be a citizen. The human type whom we should educate towards is not either 'gentleman' or 'mechanic', but rather the integrated and versatile ideal of early American and French republicanism, of English Chartism and of Scottish democracy in the last quarter of the eighteenth century and the first of the nineteenth.

In conclusion

What in fact do we have? We have a highly bureaucratized and centralized system of education both in schools and universities, nominally under local control, but in fact with little significant diversity of practice, except the great divide of the state and the private section of education; and even in the private sector there is an astounding sameness and lack of experiment. And both school systems are dominated by ideas of disciplinary attainments, little has been done to foster practical and political skills and sociability.

Also a purely office-holding, job-preserving bureaucratic assumption that all disciplines are equal, hinders both concentration and cutting down. And until we cut down in secondary education, we cannot take away the stigma of unwanted compulsion from most people's education and begin to spread resources more evenly through life. There is such a wasteful over-concentration of resources on the early years and on immediate post-school university and polytechnic, and far too little for post-experience learning at every conceivable level.

Instead of the absurd distinction of the binary policy, we should indeed have developed, even though it is an ugly word, multi-universities. The vocational and the cultural and the scientific should there have, not merged, but simply rubbed shoulders. Each student to do a little of each at least, but mostly to rub shoulders with different kinds of specialists. By limiting universities or by them limiting themselves to the scientific and the cultural, in the pattern of Humbolt's conventional disciplines, they are in danger of becoming as sterile and as irrelevant as a parliament that limited its debates to constitutional matters, ignoring the economy, production and culture; indeed worse, they are like a parliament that thinks that politics should only be practised in a parliamentary context, that sees any extra-parliamentary politics or stirrings for self-government in other fields as a threat to parliamentary democracy. Parliamentarians seem to suggest that all extra-parliamentary politics is necessarily anti-parliamentary; and universities often seem to say that any encouragement of culture and learning except through themselves is a threat. On the contrary, we need more democracy in the workshop, in the office and in the school or college; and we need more centres and devices of higher learning, other than the, at times, awful formality and laboriousness of universities and polytechnics, routines often as irrelevant to students as they are hindering to real scholars.

The polytechnic/university distinction has been mainly one of costs. But if we cannot afford such multi-purpose agglomerations as I suggest, then we should spread the costs more fairly through time, recurrent and continuing, and look again at the greatly underused asset we have of the free public library system. Rather than money for the last new university, I would have liked to have seen a new breed of tutor-librarians in each major public library to help people with self-study, and two or three small-sized meeting rooms in each library where WEA and extra-mural activities could take place. And why not self-administering neighbourhood centres of this kind, like the heavily-named 'Culture and Leisure Houses' which already exist in some German Social Democratic cities and in Israel?

Not to flinch at the post, we should also consider whether some 'education' money would not be better spent on the Arts Council grants, considering their pathetically small funding, compared to these fifty or so universities, each doing much the same kind of thing to so many who are only there for the ride or because they got three 'A' levels, or would get more out of the ride if they took it all, or even part of it, much later.

I have not really tried to apply covertly deschooling doctrines, of however mild a kind, to universities. I am only trying to remind those of us in universities and polytechnics that we do not monopolize culture and learning, and that in the interests of the whole polity we should not try to do so. Consider what threat it would be to literature if every novelist and poet could become a writer in residence or a university lecturer, as is almost universally the case in the United States. And social and political speculation have almost entirely lost their public voice now that they are social sciences and are commonly written in a jargon that you have to go to college to understand. Scientists should not be shy of their contacts with industry, if they can go back and forth; and they are, alas, sometimes right to be less than fully enthusiastic about teaching 'a normal load', if research is the thing. But we cannot justify the expense of research and pure scholarship in so very many different centres. Research is not a right of individuals, but a cultural need whose proper allocation of resources can only be settled justly in a political way, by political justice.

Ideological postscript

What I have to say about the relationship of politics to education has been coloured by the fact that I am a moderate, but a moderate socialist, not a moderate of the middle or the muddle of the whole political spectrum; and moderate, indeed, not as to ends, but only as to means.[9] Moreover if one is an idealist, in the sense of wishing to work to realise the spirit of enlightenment and the great slogans of the French Revolution, whose business is not yet finished, however often frustrated or perverted, 'Liberty, Equality, Fraternity', then one must proceed carefully, deliberately and with determination and on a long time scale. 'The man who striveth for the mastery', said Paul, 'is temperate in all things'. If he is serious, that is, and not just trendy, theatrical, using doctrine as a way of isolating him or herself from the world rather than genuinely seeking to transform it through time, instead of through visions of – to quote Dylan Thomas on the crucifixion – 'the mountain minute, time's nerve in vinegar', as if revolution like the crucifixion will qualitatively transform all human history and the possibilities of human nature.

For part of why I have written in a moderate perspective by some lights, however radical it would appear to conventional liberals, is because I believe that we should and must think in a long time scale. Most of my fellow social scientists exaggerate the uniqueness of the capitalist-industrial world. The idea of free citizenship has deeper and enduring roots in our culture; it is to be used, not transcended. And used much more. Too many socialists, indeed, seem to reject injustrialism and all concern with production, rather than trying to socialize it; they reject it either in the shamefully vague Marxist accounts of a classless society, or in the far more precise, but specifically anti-industrial, anarchist or Communard tradition of small groups and small groups only.

Heaven knows that it is not wise to destroy anything until there is something better to put in its place. But if we are ever to have a better civilization than we enjoy at the present, which is not a difficult thought, it can only come through deliberate political means, by argument, persuasion, policy and legislation, not through coercion or mystical qualitative events like revolution or conversion. And it will come, in part, through education.

Notes

[1] As I argued precisely in my first inaugural lecture at Sheffield, reprinted as 'Freedom and Politics' in my *Political Theory and Practice* (Allen Lane, 1974), and more generally in *In Defence of Politics* (Pelican Books 1976).

[2] See Hannah Arendt's *The Human Condition, On Revolution* and *On Violence* especially.

[3] Hannah Arendt, *The Human Condition*, Part II, *passim*.

[4] Bertrand de Jouvenal, 'Towards a Political Theory of Education' in *Humanistic Education and Western Civilization: Essays for Robert M. Hutchins*, edited by Arthur A. Cohen, (New York, 1964), p. 67.

[5] *Ibid.*, p. 68.

[6] The Green Paper of 1977, *Education in Schools: a Consultative Document* (Cmnd. 6869) only wishes to discuss 'with their partners in the education service' (i.e. all LEA's) the possibility of agreement on a common core (para. 2.19), with no apparent assertion of any national interest (devolution and separatism are not mentioned), only as if a common core is purely a matter of slow and voluntary reform of certain subject areas for their own sake. The whole section on 'Action on the curriculum' (paras. 2.18–2.23) is weak as to make one wonder if all sense of the State has been lost; and if what is left is only agreement between local and central bureaucracies.

[7] Jouvenal, *op. cit*, p. 69.

[8] When George Orwell thought, in his *The Lion and The Unicorn* (first published 1941, reprinted 1962), that a social revolution was taking place as a consequence of the war, he said that 'Most of its directing brains will come from the new indeterminate class of skilled workers, technical experts, airmen, scientists, architects and journalists, the people who feel at home in the radio and ferro-concrete age' (pp. 85–6). Orwell saw no inconsistency in valuing both literary culture and common culture.

[9] See my 'The Character of a Moderate (Socialist)', *The Political Quarterly*, January 1976.

PART TWO

The Social Implications

4. Continuing Education for Social Decision-makers

Robert Houlton

Introduction

In examining the social implications of continuing education, most of the emphasis in this chapter will be on the education of voluntary social decision-makers. This should not be seen as overlooking the real and legitimate claims that can be made for cultural adult education, from baroque music to pop, from the painters of the Renaissance to modern comic book heroes. Indeed, the failure of adult education to match its 'high' cultural offerings in the area of university extra-mural education with a similar investment of resources in popular culture is worthy of analysis.

But in a country where the claims of failure, wasted years and lost opportunities have been the currency of politicians for over three decades, it is appropriate to examine the contribution which continuing education could and should make to voluntary social decision-making. Most of the data in this chapter will be drawn from industry in general and shop steward education in particular. But many of the insights and procedures outlined would be matched by anyone who has taught on community, citizen's rights, or magistrates' courses. While the focus may be specific, it is hoped that some conclusions may have a wider validity.

A learning situation

For seven years from 1969–77, as a Lecturer in Economics and Industrial Studies at the University of Liverpool, I taught the shop stewards from the Ford Motor Company plant and a host of other Merseyside companies. These courses provided *my* major learning experience during this period and still provide an important datum point in my thinking about the present and future role of adult education. I see no value in concealing this auto-biographical reference although I realize that it could make my perceptions suspect and my conclusions dubious to some of my readers. For those who haven't taught a group of shop stewards, I would like to describe the context and the processes involved.

Three times a year fifteen to twenty tough bargainers would crowd into a classroom at the Royal Institution, six hours a day for ten consecutive weeks. Within half an hour of starting the atmosphere would be blue with cigarette smoke. In that time the tutor would have been challenged. The nature of the challenge varied. Sometimes he would be asked to interpret a current industrial dispute, or a previous day's government announcement. At other times the challenge would be about course content or organization. What was happening, in effect, was that the tutor was required to re-establish his credentials, and parade his competence and credibility. If this first hurdle was not successfully overcome, there were likely to be problems for the rest of the day. The sessions were tough on tutor and student alike. Many students would say 'It's worse than working.' But during a course a vast amount of knowledge would be exchanged, assessed and either incorporated or rejected. Although the tutor was both a resource and a catalyst, much of the process, pattern and pace of learning was in the hands of the students themselves. They presented their demands for information, for analytical concepts and for learning skills to the tutor – they were skilled bargainers, after all. The course programme was therefore continually being negotiated around the basic parameters of

1. the agreed syllabus
2. the limited resources available, especially time
3. the students' different interests.

It is impossible for any participant, especially a tutor, to offer an objective assessment of such a simultaneously nerve-racking and rewarding experience. However, the SIT Hutchinson's Industrial Studies Series and the BBC Television Adult Education Series 'On Union Business' provide some evidence of the strange fruit which germinated in this adult education hot-house. Although the process of adult education was difficult, the industrial tutor had the advantage of a disturbed social environment outside the classroom.

Industrial studies and social change

One should remember that the decade from 1967–77 was probably the most dramatic in the history of British industrial relations. In those years the established institutions of British trade unionism struggled to incorporate the grass roots shop stewards' movement into the formal procedures of bargaining. Shop stewards' organizations had previously been regarded by many full-time union officials as quasi-outlaw phenomena.

Shop stewards who tried to set up communication links in the late 1950s and early 1960s between the different plants of the same company were often harried by personnel managers and full-time union officials alike. By the mid-1960s it was increasingly clear that this policy was not only futile but also possibly counter-productive. But the failure of the unions to incorporate effectively their shop floor representatives brought in the active intervention of the Labour and Conservative governments and attempts to use legislation to regulate voluntary behaviour. The State itself was attempting to impose a new pattern of incorporation on the trade unions. By the end of the 1970s it appears that this agonising social adjustment is virtually complete. A new generation of trade union officials is prepared to recognize the legitimacy of the shop steward's role in industry, though with reservations.

Trade unions have come to realize that the alternative to parliamentary legislation is judge-made law, and many prefer the former given a substantial trade union representation in the House of Commons and House of Lords. The State has also made adjustments. As the established element in the 'governance' of the country, civil service has developed a Pavlovian response to established trade unionism. On most new industrial, economic or advisory committees, the TUC is automatically represented together with what Whitehall sees as the main sparring partner, the ubiquitous CBI. Members of Parliament, the 'temps' of governance, still exhibit a certain ambivalence to trade unionism. No doubt some are fearful of the trade union movement's demonstrated ability to react negatively and frustrate or destroy legislation. Others remain unconvinced about the TUC General Council's willingness and ability to adopt and support policies in the national interest.

All MPs however, have to accept that the participation of the TUC was essential to the survival of the Wilson–Callaghan administration and crucial for the success of the first and second stages of the Social Contract in the mid-1970s. As the British trade union movement exhibits simultaneously conservative and radical behavioural traits, many back bench MPs must wonder whether they have chosen the right institution in which to display their talents.

These have been dramatic times in industrial relations which have guaranteed the motivation and interest of shop stewards on industrial studies courses. Some seemingly parochial industrial disputes have travelled through the political system to land on the desks of cabinet ministers. Shop stewards from Ford's could quote *verbatim* what Barbara Castle, the Minister for Employment, had said when she met the sewing room girls when they were on unofficial strike for equal pay. Clydeside shipyard workers not only gained access to the Prime Minister's drawing room but also refused his whisky. There was a realization by many shop stewards that they were part of an industrial system that could be highly unstable. For example, a technical malfunction in a paint-spray booth could trigger a chain of events resulting in 50,000 ceasing to work, lost production running into millions of pounds, a slump in share prices, and a neurotic flight of the holders of sterling into another currency. Could Athens, Sparta, Rome, St. Petersburg, Berlin, London or Washington at different times in history have offered a more dramatic role to men and women who had been born in poverty, raised in deprivation and had experienced what was, for many, mindless toil since leaving school?

Contemporary 'higher' and 'lower' adult education

The contrast between trade union students and the limp Economic History undergraduates or the anxiously-conformist Master of Business Administration post-graduates I taught could not have been greater. Shop stewards generally were a group of socially deprived decision-makers, selected through peer-group election, who were tackling a stressful role on a voluntary basis, and in some cases losing earnings as a result. But they were avid learners, willing to examine any form of knowledge and to test its relevance on the shop floor. They would go to great lengths to share knowledge and help each other through difficulties. Their whole tradition of social solidarity was harnessed to learning. At the same time these same students remained independent, very much their own men or women and resolutely critical of the educational process and to anything they considered 'brainwashing'.

The behaviour and attitude of the under- and post-graduates were completely different. Most of them took a simple competitive and instrumental view of the learning process. As a group they were vastly more introverted and less secure than the stewards, having been schooled to look for 'right' rather than alternative answers to problems. If the majority had a spark of creativity or insight, they took care to keep it hidden. In place of a robust critical attitude, theirs was an oscillation between apathy and cynicism. Most industrial tutors would, I think, confirm that many of the privileged beneficiaries of public investment in higher education display an unwillingness to think for themselves and a limited capacity for original or creative thought in a group situation. What they *have* developed, however, is an ability to compete effectively in formal examinations. This is something which many shop stewards, even after two years of full-time residential adult education, find extremely difficult to do. This is another indication that current formal examination systems provide limited evidence of all-round intellectual abilities: for obvious reasons they cannot provide any valid indication of the way in which these abilities would be used in a given social context. It is a commonplace but relevant indictment of the educational system that it has stripped the learning process out of its social context and that it has carried specialization beyond the point of coherence.

The case of the vertical slide rule

Any industrial studies course 'discovers' intellectual talent which has been 'hidden' from the educational system. One example of the intellectual abilities of an ex-secondary modern 'C' stream shop steward was Tony Drew, a semi-skilled Ford's shop steward who worked on the wet-deck, rubbing down the bare steel bodies of cars before they were painted with primer. Tony gave the impression of being slow and had been called Ticky at school because, it was said, he was as 'tick as two short planks'. He was a self-confessed intellectual failure. Yet Tony enjoyed the respect of all his fellow-workers and shop stewards, which suggested either that any abilities he had were usually concealed or that he had been a late developer. One day they came to the surface. The course was being introduced to the slide rule and as a preliminary everyone was making a simple binary calculator with ruled paper, and moving them from side to side in multiplication using log base two. Then Ticky Tony Drew dropped his bombshell. 'Tell me,' he said, 'Why does a slide rule go from side to side instead of up and down?'

1	2	4	8	16	32	64	128	256	512				
1	2	4	8	16	32	64	128	256	512	1024	2048	4096·	8192

When faced with an unusual question the best technique is to play for time.

'Why do you ask, Tony?'

'Well,' he said in a thick Scouse accent, 'If it went up and down you'd be able to see better and multiply much bigger numbers.' And he held up his vertical slide rule to make his point.

Within ten minutes everyone was making giant vertical binary slide rules.

Since that time I've discovered that the question 'Why don't we have vertical slide rules so that we can read the numbers more easily?' is guaranteed to halt most scientists in mid-sentence. Of course, Tony Drew's insight was not unique. One of the most accurate slide rules, the Otis King Calculator, does operate on a vertical principle.

Out of this incident the shop stewards course launched into an extended discussion of the way in which calculating and measuring instruments determine not only thought processes but also social organizations. This ran the gamut from the current campaign by many workers to make all the time clocks in the factory 'inoperative' to the way in which many white-

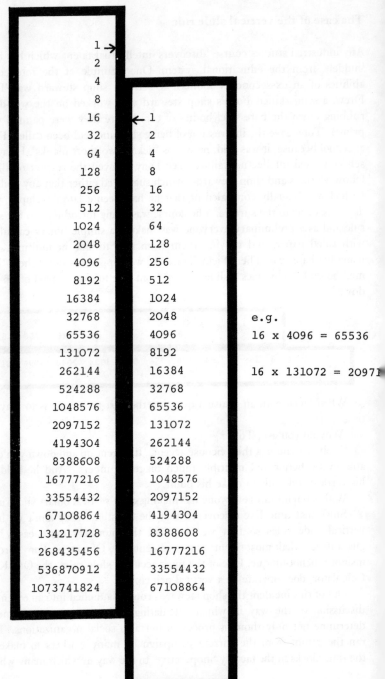

1 →		
2		
4		
8		
16	← 1	
32	2	
64	4	
128	8	
256	16	
512	32	
1024	64	
2048	128	
4096	256	
8192	512	
16384	1024	
32768	2048	e.g.
65536	4096	16 x 4096 = 65536
131072	8192	
262144	16384	16 x 131072 = 20971
524288	32768	
1048576	65536	
2097152	131072	
4194304	262144	
8388608	524288	
16777216	1048576	
33554432	2097152	
67108864	4194304	
134217728	8388608	
268435456	16777216	
536870912	33554432	
1073741824	67108864	

collar technicians deliberately build a mystique around their instruments and techniques. The vocabulary and concepts may have been commonplace but the insight was at times extraordinary. However, it is generally true in industrial adult education that intense direct personal experience subjected to reflective thought processes is a more than adequate substitute for the intellectual training presently offered in many areas of higher education.

There is also another, more disturbing conclusion that can be drawn from industrial studies courses, namely, that the British education system systematically screens out potential 'natural' decision-makers. Instead of providing challenge and opportunity to the hyperactive extrovert, the school system seeks to control, contain, divert and frustrate them. The result is that higher education does not provide the entrepreneurs, the questers, the agents of change that British society so urgently requires. Instead, in many instances, the natural decision-makers surface in their late twenties and early thirties when their fellow-workers recognize their leadership qualities and elect them as shop stewards. In this social context their initial role is to resist rather than promote change. A number, however, transcend their initiation into decision-making and eventually supply a level of leadership on the shop floor and in the local community which managers signally fail to provide.

A few cross the cultural and organizational frontier to take on management roles – despite the common accusation that they have 'sold out'. It is the nature of this frontier dividing those who give orders from those who have to carry them out to which our attention must be turned.

Modelling social roles

In order to model and understand social and organizational roles it is necessary to appreciate a number of basic distinctions. The primary one is the difference between the *professional* decision-maker, whose job and role coincide, and the voluntary decision-maker, the *activist*, whose job and role are different. The professional decision-maker often operates under a pressure that the activist rarely feels. A perennial complaint by the professional about the activist – manager about shop steward, civil servant about politician, local government officer about councillor, policeman about magistrate and clergyman about laity – is that they lack expertise and commitment. However, given the ease of 'dropping out', it is a wonder that voluntary decision-makers are present in such numbers in a society which has become increasingly professionalized. Both professional and activist are subject to a similar set of constraints, namely: *limited time, limited resources, limited enthusiasm*, and *limiting commitments*. These constraints can easily be overlooked by adult educators in their missionary zeal but they are the parameters within which all social activities take place.

A second important factor to be considered in relation to social decision-making is the position of the decision-maker both in time and in relation to the policy being pursued. On many major issues the key decision – the initiation or otherwise of action – is the prerogative of the 'insider'. The 'outsider' is inevitably in the position of reacting to a prior decision, although the outsider's decision may be positive and in support of the insider's decision. It is tempting to carry through the distinction by making the shop steward the reactionary 'outsider' to positive 'insider' management decisions. But in some situations managers are the outsiders to trade union decisions. The insider-outsider polarity depends on (a) the context, (b) the issue and (c) the time scale. It is important to remember that 'insiders', whether trade unionists or managers, cannot operate without a degree of autonomy and there are inevitably limits to the degree of participation in joint decision-making by groups with different areas of autonomy. Even so one should recognize that there is a permanent 'insider' infrastructure in industry and central and local government manned by managers, permanent civil servants and local government officers. This 'insider' infrastructure generates its own ideology and at social gatherings this is manifested in ritual calls about the state of the country, the quality of members of the current government or local council, and the damage, real or potential, that voluntary or quasi-voluntary groups are doing to the national fabric.

It is tempting for reasons of symmetry alone to adopt Galbraith's concept of countervailing power and suggest that a countervailing outsider infrastructure exists which matches, debates and, at times, confronts the managerial bureaucratic insider infrastructure. However, to do so would be to imply a coherence and a continuity which, in fact, is conspicuous by its absence. Outsider groups are fragmented in their perceptions, and divided in their policies and ideologies. Temporary coalitions can be formed but as group solidarity is a prime consideration, and the loss of membership to other groups is an ever-present threat, inter-group competitive tensions are usually present. And such coalitions are vulnerable to social control by the selective incorporation of some of the leaders and the granting of real or symbolic insider status.

There can be all kinds of permutations of the insider/outsider dichotomy depending on the social system being examined and its characteristics. It is useful, however, to focus on British society as a whole, while remembering that the national perspective may conceal many important variations at the local and regional level.

One of the forces shaping national attitudes is the mass media, recognisably one of the all-pervading instruments of social education in modern society, setting agenda, placing selective emphasis on some issues and ignoring others. One of the permanent themes within the media is the preservation of continuity, order and the maintenance of the social fabric – in other words, the preoccupations of the central insider structure. The activities of outsiders and voluntary groups usually become newsworthy when they are seen to be disruptive. I am not making the often repeated (and justified) charge of bias against trade unions. Very few voluntary groups get responsible news coverage. The Royal Society of Medicine, to take a recent example, only becomes newsworthy when there is dissension within its membership and the President resigns. The achievements of the RSM over the past 170 years have gone relatively unreported by the media. Of course, outsider groups being dependent on a voluntary membership are 'open' organizations, their problems are more exposed to public scrutiny than insider organizations.

It is little wonder that all activist organizations worry about member involvement, apathy and the general antipathetic attitude of members of the public. This must, in part, be due to the powerful negative conditioning which people receive from the mass media and the widespread currency of the phrase 'never volunteer!' Despite this, Britain is still alive with voluntary societies, either registered under trades union legislation (which includes Employers' Societies) or the Industrial and Provident Societies Acts. Under the surveillance of the Registrar of Friendly Societies there exists a bewildering variety of sports, social and recreational clubs, agricultural societies, fishing societies, learned societies, productive societies and service societies. Each society is grounded on the voluntary principle and has to find a solution to the tension between member/activists and the professionals.

The range of problems that the legion of voluntary societies confront and solve extends across the whole spectrum of academic learning; from the social sciences, the physical sciences, law and medicine. But where, how and when do they engage with the institutions of learning? Overall the relationship is haphazard. Those organizations which were concerned with working-class emancipation in the nineteenth and early twentieth century saw a need to educate their members both in basic organizational techniques and, to a lesser extent, the wider social issues. As a result the procedural operations of many trade unions and consumer co-operative societies are extremely efficient. Indeed, to some extent the skills of chairmanship and committee procedure have been pursued as ends in themselves. In middle-class voluntary societies the lack of such skills is often depressingly obvious

83

as committees are 'led by the nose' by the dominant member and decisions are unerringly avoided. On the other hand, in contrast to middle-class groups, working-class voluntary groups generally lack creativity and are not innovators.

Different voluntary groups have different educational and training needs – so any would-be adult education missionary foraging in this area should be aware that standard packages cannot be applied to different groups without modification.

Implications

Clearly it is possible to envisage a broad programme of continuing education for social decision-makers, though it is difficult to establish the long-term effective demand. The trade union movement is an obvious segment with 300,000 workplace representatives and 150,000 branch representatives (many of them being the same people in different roles). Even with the greatly expanded programme of TUC shop steward day-release courses it is unlikely that more than ten per cent of this market is being reached. The need for TUC courses is obvious to anyone familiar with industry. It is not unusual for the most vocal critic of the trade union to be elected a shop steward. This means that problems are being confronted by a repre-sentative without any prior experience in decision-making or negotiating. Many shop stewards are unsure how the shop floor organization links and relates via the branch to the formal structure of the union. The induction and education of shop stewards within an accepted pattern of courses is essential if a civilized working environment is to be maintained in industry.

Another sector of the Labour Movement which depends on voluntary activists is Retail Co-operative Societies with about 60,000 out of a member-ship of 10 million. The Co-operative Movement's lay leadership accept a tradition of hierarchical progression through committees which usually ensures that activists have 'served their time' before they reach the effective centres of decision-making. While informal education continually takes place, the total involvement in formal education again is probably about four per cent.

For the other sectors one can only speculate. Perhaps 60,000 activists are involved in running social, entertainment and recreational clubs. The Working Men's Club and Institute Union provides correspondence courses and weekend schools. For this sector and the producer, agricultural and fishing societies it would be impossible, without research, to identify the proportion of activists who would benefit from a continuing education provision. But these are worth investigation and perhaps investment.

Britain as a society still retains faith in the value of democracy and social integration and, by and large, both are reflected in voluntary organizations.

Would the voluntary sector welcome increased involvement in formal education? Who knows? Given the strong tradition of self-help, a social solidarity which tends to reject non-members even from élites, and the fear of competition for the time of active members, it is unlikely that the floodgates will suddenly open. But if a genuine collaborative partnership could be established it might benefit the education, the society and the activist alike. The experience of industrial tutors is eloquent testimony to this possibility.

5. Towards a Sociology of Universal Higher Education

Colin Fletcher

Sociology tells us that the law in relation to citizens' rights rarely matches those same citizens' beliefs. Instead, the law is behind, or in advance of, culture. In effect, law-makers catch up with the times or push forward to change attitudes by changing the activities permitted. In the case of universal higher education both propositions would seem to apply. Work people's representatives are demanding, by negotiation, paid educational leave. Technological changes and the complexity of everyday life are making it necessary for adults to be trained and educated at frequent intervals throughout their life. In fact, one of the few points of ready agreement between educators, employers and employees would appear to be the need for universal higher education. A crude sociological sketch would show that conflicts would centre upon the content and purposes. Educators favour liberal education, employers think in terms of training and employees reason along the lines of their collective strength in struggles with their employers.

It is possible, therefore, to suggest that universal higher education divides neatly into three kinds of provision: liberal courses, vocational training and trade union studies. This would mean simply extending the availability of existing provision and shoring up the support given to adults whilst in receipt. The contention in this paper is, however, that a qualitative change is imminent that brings with it a host of new possibilities and implications. A sociology of universal higher education would begin with propositions about people's rights and relate these to their circumstances. The hub of the argument is quite simply that the past may not be of great value in charting the future and that the present embodies many inequalities which the crude division of present provision serves partly to sustain. Thus a sociology of universal adult education would propose that the present provisions are left untouched and that will and effort are devoted to the alternatives which the goal would suggest. The drift of this paper is, therefore, not to take issue with the present arrangements but to assume that the goal is worthy of fresh initiatives which, taken together, are well in advance of people's beliefs. In sum, changes in actions would give the term 'universal higher education' direct and diverse meanings. Throughout, however, the implications are looked at through a sociologist's eyes and are biased in this respect.

86

Action one: paid educational leave as an employee's right

ILO Convention 140 gives work people the right of between 8 and 14 days of leave with pay each year to be able to 'receive' education. After careful study of the forms which this entitlement might take this could become part of the legal rights and responsibilities of the employee; paid educational leave would be 'put on the statute book'.

The phrase 'the forms which this entitlement might take' conceals a number of hazards and heart-searchings. Approximately one-quarter of all employees work shifts and only exact specification would make day-time courses possible for them. Even then permanent night-shift workers would need special arrangements.

It can be safely assumed that larger firms would find the conditions easier to satisfy. Their premises might also become venues for the employees of small businesses. Local consortia comparable with Industrial Training Boards could be encouraged. Much would depend upon the terms determined with regard to age-strata and the content of courses.

To take the latter first, educationalists would insist, one suspects, on an element of liberal education and take issue with a purely task-related or company-based provision. The consequence would be to blur the terms teacher and trainer and the bodies to whom such people were primarily responsible. A large efficient firm would have little trouble in translating the entitlement into that of viewing slides of its world-wide operations and giving insights into its accounting procedures. The owner of a small business, on the other hand, might cast about for a sub-contracting teacher and be disturbed about the slant given to current issues. At the very least, sectors of state education are less well prepared than some parts of private and state corporations. However it may be viewed, the initial period would be a golden opportunity for the entrepreneur and the manufacturers of packaged learning.

Throughout, too, there is an assumption of the relative passivity of the adult learner. It is as if men and women are likely to be cautiously attentive and reticent. This assumption is not met by the experiences of industrial tutors as Robert Houlton has tellingly shown in the preceding chapter. It is not so much a matter of teaching and breaking off for discussion but of pointed discussion with the force to break the teacher before he or she has got round to the text for the day. The acute problem is that adult teaching is not a minor modification of orthodox secondary education. At its best an adult class is voluntary, eclectic, egalitarian and alive to current affairs. Progressive comprehensive education may well aspire to the same qualities but the teachers of teachers do not seem to have kept up with developments.

Part Two: The Social Implications

Again, the state sector would find that paid educational leave put demand upon it for which little preparation has been made.

The truth is that from the very beginning the right to paid educational leave would be visible as, in part, being a set of restrictions. Use was made of the ugly term 'age-strata'. The term implies that the right would be limited to those under a certain age. Hungarian legislation, for example, extends the right to men and women under 45 years of age. It is possible that those over the age of 45 might have the right to education for retirement but is unlikely to amount to an average of ten days a year for fifteen years; unlikely but not impossible.

Although paid educational leave is treated as a discrete action it does relate to the more experimental action of establishing the right of adults, especially parents, to attend school classes.

Action two: the right of adults to attend schools

If the broadest meaning of paid educational leave were taken it would include parents going to their children's classes registered and paid accordingly. This attendance (though without payment) already happens in some secondary schools and preliminary findings are instructive.

In the first instance parents seem to enrol in different classes from their children whilst grandparents enrol in the same classes as their young. Initially too, scholastic courses can be more daunting and a preference expressed for practical subjects. Adults and children then mix and their relationship with the teacher does not depend upon either fear or favouritism.

The major problem is that of respective spans of interest. The adult may expect a period of clear instruction and a project or enquiry which takes some time to satisfactorily solve. The young persons may prefer the opposite with greater independence from the teacher and making a briefer effort before getting results. Thus in no sense do adults simply 'join in' classes and nor should they be expected to do. In fact only in the case of courses leading to qualifications could adults and young persons be 'treated the same'.

It should be apparent that there is some wavering between the terms adults and parents, children and young persons. Dealing with the former, parents could have a right to learn with their children in 'family sessions' and all classes could be potentially 'family sessions'. By this it is meant that evening classes could also be extended to include a number of young people and relatives. Where this has been tried it appears that the preponderance during the day remains that of young people and in the evening that of adults. The presence of other adults appears to inhibit undue anxiety about

88

a particular relationship as well as afford the possibility of others. This generalization seems especially apt when those 'unattached adults' are in the eighteen to thirty age group and so bridge the two main generations.

So far it has not proved the case that most of the parents are women. More obvious is the fact that either both parents 'return to school' or neither do, and it is the 'unattached adults' that are more often women. In most cases they are adults, parents and workers. It should be apparent, however, that this right would offer greater equality as well as opportunity to adults. It means that those who are self-employed or non-employed gain some access equivalent to paid educational leave. The disadvantage of not being paid can only be understood alongside the disadvantages of the same groups not being paid for so many other activities either.

No end of problems can be foreseen if the action were to be extended by principle rather than committed practice. Again, many teachers are ill-prepared and fear hostile, or even mild criticism. Their unions could well make teacher-pupil ratios an issue and demand fewer children in the class should adults be included. In the latter case even more problems would occur if the adults were not obliged to attend at a particular time. It has been found that occasional attendance can be met with 'pay as you learn' (on the spot payments for actual sessions) but this may only solve a problem if the previous issues are in abeyance or resolved. This would not be an easy action for those with a legalistic frame of mind.

Action three: free courses in 'civics'

A working assumption in many branches of adult education is that it is a self-financing activity. No payment is often required, though, from the unemployed, chronically sick, elderly or illiterate. The last category raises an important principle because rather than being based upon the ability to pay it depends upon an ability being seen as a right. Adult illiterates are not expected to pay for their tuition partly because of the low costs with voluntary tutors and partly because the tuition is making up for an opportunity lost whilst of a school age. Somewhere between the notion of 'ability' and 'lost opportunity' occurs political awareness in the broadest sense.

Adult educators face the fact that current affairs, national and international issues invariably came to their classes' attention through television. They are also aware of the pockets of attitudes that are associated with many controversies. Beliefs are rarely thought through; many are fatalistic or just forlorn. Knowledge of institutions may be similarly patchy particularly in relation to the machinery of government.

Part Two: The Social Implications

These observations are not offered because this is 'a deplorable state of affairs' but because being an adult means an increasing burden of responsibilities and need for competence. 'Civics' is simply an expansive term to describe a working knowledge of the factors affecting everyday life and how to have an effect, directly or indirectly, upon them. That these courses would be free is a recognition of the extent of 'lag' in awareness and the gravity of the situation. And without wishing to draft a syllabus from ecology to energy through to the economy it would seem that there is a lot to be learned from the Scandanavian commitment to a grasp of domestic politics. No doubt every conceivable course could be soundly criticized for being too parochial or too ecumenical in content. As much at issue is the form such study would take.

Most adults prefer to do something and think about it at the same time (Champion 1975 a). There is sound sense in this because the separation of work and worry can be a source of anxiety in itself. Consequently all adult classes which involve learning how to do something by doing it tend to run purposefully from beginning to end. 'Civics' may, therefore, be taught more successfully by workshops and the occasional formal public lecture. A workshop is no more than a practical session which involves in this case searching for and organizing information and then simplifying it to essentials. WEA Classes on local history and local living conditions serve to indicate the research potential of a well-tutored class. At some point adults have to grapple with all that the barbarous phrase 'communications technology' implies. At the very least publishing and television have to be seen from the inside out. Workshops would, therefore, work to some purpose. One goal would be to produce some useful material. Ideally there would not be endless repetition in each locality.

The problem, when it is faced, is that there is so much to do. Evidence from experimental and free health education shows that people are reached who have not previously been reached before. There is no suggestion here that civics and health education are directly comparable. The point is that they both have to do with dealing with contemporary life and that people are concerned as well as curious. Health education 'classes' have been unusually large.

Action four: extend the community education aspects of every centre

Community education in this context means the outreach programme of semi-directed activities; it means the 'teachers' going out of their 'centres' to other places of public assembly and creating the circumstances in which people can learn close to where they can live. Traditional LEA adult education has thrived on this principle for decades using primary schools, public and church halls. Projects in Liverpool extended their work to clubs and pubs (Lovett).

In fact, of course, all three previous 'actions' have depended upon accepting centres of learning; the works' canteen or apprentice school; the adult education centre and the secondary school. The assumption is partly that the activity is recognizable as 'education' and partly that the place in which it happens is recognizably a place of learning. This assumption has to be challenged because so many adults recall school with loathing and look upon the new steel and glass centres with considerable trepidation. The truth is that they have no intention of going in them but they are quite happy to talk with those who work in them *outside*.

In this action it is not the case of adult education 'plugging gaps' in secondary education but 'healing wounds'. Adults fresh to adult education continuously anticipate rejection and are highly susceptible to chance remarks. Being on their home ground may help in this respect but it does not suspend disbelief entirely. The root belief is 'you want me to think that I want to do something; you want me to do something for reasons you are not telling me'. Most community education outreach programmes have met this problem acutely when they have tried to maintain chance contacts and aroused people's worst fears. In brief, in community education of this nature, the strains are almost entirely upon the teachers.

Community education activities run into the same problems as might be anticipated for civics courses. To educate, strengthen and even ennoble a part of the community is to encourage informal leaders and disturb local arrangements, particularly those that relate to housing. It is a rare education indeed that has no effect and in both cases some attention is focused upon present conditions. Neighbourhood centres are best understood as a meeting point of houses and the homes they provide. There is no point in pretending that community education does not puncture and deflate the belief that invariably nothing ever gets done. Just the opposite may happen and has happened. Close on the heels of community education projects have come improvements and rehousing. The problems and tensions increase but the causes change. In fact community education in relation to tenants' and residents' associations may be already an intrinsic part of a process of accelerated change in areas with 'housing problems'. What is clear, however, is that different educational topics are in focus and the teacher's role is closer to that of the adult-in-contact than it is in any of the other alternatives (Claxton 1973).

Part Two: The Social Implications

Action five: recognize the relevance to adult education of voluntary groups and recreational organizations

It is hard to see the point of extending the hand of friendship when it is apparently not needed. The question at issue is, though, not that of friendship but facilities. All manner of groups struggle to find somewhere to meet at considerable cost and with varying degrees of security. Schools remain firmly closed to them because they are not truly adult education and the supervision of their use does not 'come under adult education'. The proper response might be 'form yourselves into a class' but this is a matter of adjusting the lens rather than the reality.

Recognition is an action in this respect because it entails carrying out more duties. The potential is that of recognizing that voluntary bodies like drama groups, musicians and choirs form and flourish because they have somewhere to practice and perform. It is not a matter of taking them over but of adult education extending to being a housekeeper of adult welfare and expressly so where few or no other facilities exist. The principle does suggest that schools become adult education centres for more than *bona fide* classes with a minimum of enrolment. In effect the strong element of independent learning in adult education is extended to recognizing self-education in *bona fide* groups. This action, like the one which follows, could be called a formality of commonsense.

Action six: a local counselling service and information point

Some adults may be facing financial hardships and harsh conditions. Others may wish to learn a hobby or keep their minds active. Yet others may be faced with truncated careers and the need for new qualifications. And whilst the sectors of adult education work in isolation it is clear that advertising and enrolment nights present a bewildering range of choices. Consequently chances can be wasted, classes can fail to run and the adults concerned reject the system entirely. Already at some centres the adults can discuss before they decide, and sample for a trial period without obligation. Those who wish to go quickly can attend two classes a week whilst those who would rather find their own pace can attend one class a week. It would seem that the emphasis placed upon counselling as to what is available and the commitment the courses entail satisfies the adult students in that they do not drop out at anything like the normal rate (Champion 1975 *b*).

There is no need for an administration of this service. The expectation is that the provisions are mutually understood by the existing services and that they share their evening's work rather than separate as if to different sections of the population. In practice this action might prove the most idealistic because it involves changes in the 'management' of adult education as distinct from 'bigger productions' in its many theatres. Power has moved further and further away from the centre's principals and tutors and been drawn to regional controllers. Perhaps this shift has enabled adult education to cheerfully survive thus far. But be that as it may, centralized power does not enable the best broad service for local people which is the guiding principle behind this action.

Reflections upon the actions discussed

The sociological imagination has proved singularly contentious with respect to cherished institutions and their defences. It has also failed to do more than hint at the real substance of the actions which when taken together go some way towards higher education for all. It must be recalled that it was not the intention to discuss successors to liberal education, training and trade union studies. Nor was it intended to exclude higher education by raising the school leaving age, Dip HEs or legions of mature students in Universities and Polytechnics. All of these categories do, however, depend essentially upon the adult becoming a student – except the school leaving-age issue which depends upon the student beginning as a child and leaving as an adult! What has been discussed here is essentially more ordinary and has been to do with adults as workers, parents and activists of all kinds. It is this aspect of the ordinary adult which demands closer reasoning.

To be 'for all' implies to be equally between the sexes, proportionally between the ages and of sufficient variety to provide each person with a point of engagement. Yet this puts the matter in administrative rather than social terms. Collectively it would seem that the actions constitute 'positive discrimination', they are biased towards working-class adults. This point should be obvious because the majority of the adult population are working-class but it does put the politics of universal adult education into sharp relief. Education is a matter of expending effort before the returns can be shown. Education also begs the question of returns for whom. Great emphasis has been placed here on benefiting the adults concerned. It must be accepted that socially education has two consequences which refract differently; educated people are also critical people; conflicts can be both clarified and contained. Thus it is not suggested that sociological analysis predicts major social change as a consequence of higher education for all. Perhaps free civics courses would help environmental protestors and amenity campaigners. It is possible that paid educational leave would raise the consciousness of the employees to question relations of labour and capital.

Part Two: The Social Implications

Yet these prognostications have more to do with specific hopes and fears.

The root changes, if 'positive discrimination' is taken as the overarching principle of the six actions, have to do with higher education itself. At the very point of contact between root hair and soil the 'teacher' would become a term to describe an army of adults. Comparatively few teachers would be solely concerned with young children. The exclusion of the right of adults to attend schools would, therefore, have side-stepped this possibly disturbing point of view. As it was included, an important aspect of higher education for all becomes the superficially contradictory outcome of adults having a firm place in schools at all times and in a whole manner of ways.

Historically adult educators have had good reason to be wary of schools. Even now the articulate preference is for separate sites and funds and those who know the present work are sympathetic to this view. The feeling is that 'school people' talk at you not with you and this may often be the case. The conjectures here have to do with schools learning to accept adults whilst a barrage of reforms puts adult interests first. If anything then, the debating point also returns to the twin poles of youth/adult, compulsory attendance/ voluntary attendance. Interestingly, paid educational leave has aspects of all four points; is by far the singly most important action towards a charter for modern men and women; and would be a matter of matching a change in beliefs rather than stimulating such a change with provisions.

In no sense, however, should the actions discussed be seen as compensating for a necessary decline in the existing pattern of provision. In fact the warning note of 'irreparable damage' sounded by Mee and Wiltshire (1977) should be responded to with the utmost urgency; the formation of local Adult Education and Training Advisory Services (Bacon *et al* 1977) could run parallel with opinion surveys (Thompson and Beggs 1977) to coordinate provision and pressure; the needs of the disabled have not been mentioned explicitly as an action imperative either (Flint *et al*). The point is that the slogan 'Higher Education for All' stimulates thrusts beyond defensive improvements of the present activities which may, in turn, reveal the good reasons why they cannot be jettisoned in the pursuit of well-intentioned but barely-tested possibilities.

References

BACON, A.W., WELLINGS A., REDMOND, M. (1977) 'Extending Adult Education' in *Adult Education* vol. 50 no. 1 14–20.

CHAMPION, Alan (1975 *a*) 'Towards an Ontology in Adult Education' in *Studies in Adult Education* vol. 7 no. 1 16–24. It will be apparent that the approach through culture and actions presupposes a dialogue between providers on the issue of needs/wants: characteristics/intentions.

CHAMPION, Alan (*b*) 'On Pilgrim College and Blackfriars' Mimeo, October 1975.

CLAXTON, C.W. 'Identifying Community Needs'. Report of a conference arranged by the East Midlands Regional Institute of Adult Education for professionals working in the field of adult/community education and held at Nottingham University on 6 March 1973.

FLINT, R., WELLS, J.H., VERNON, G. 'Adult Education and the Disabled Student' in *Adult Education*, vol. 50 no. 1 29–34.

LOVETT, T.O., in *Studies in Adult Education* vol. 3 no. 1 2–14 publishes an abridged version of 'Community Adult Education', evidence submitted to the Russell Committee on Adult Education in England and Wales by the Workers' Educational Association ('West Lancashire and District) and the Liverpool Educational Priority Area Action/Research Project.

THOMPSON, B. and BEGGS, A., (1977) 'Opinion Surveys: a means of learning and evaluating in adult education' in *The Vocational Aspects of Education* vol. 29 no. 72 31–36.

WILTSHIRE, H.C., and MEE, G. (1977) *Structure and Performance in Adult Education* Longman.

PART THREE

The Economic Implications

6. The Problems of Financing Higher Education

Gareth Williams

Different models of universal higher education

It is not without reason that economics came to be known as the dismal science. There is nothing that dampens enthusiasm for promising new ideas more than asking how much it will cost and who will pay for it. More good ideas have probably come to grief through a failure to give honest answers to these questions than any other reason. Certainly no expansion of public sector activities can be envisaged in the 1980s without facing up to the questions of cost and financing. To condemn the economist because he happens to be the person who formulates the questions that are inherent in any resource-consuming activity is rather like the ancient Greek practice of killing the messenger who brought bad tidings.

It is easy to be enthusiastic about higher education for all – particularly if you hope to be earning your living by helping to provide it. It is less easy to see who will be willing to pay for it. At the level of propaganda there is one glib answer. If we are entering a period in which unemployment levels are likely to be considerably higher than those we have grown used to since 1945, there is in one sense virtually no cost in enrolling people in higher education as an alternative to enforced idleness. What could be more tempting than to pay student grants to men (and women) out of work rather than unemployment benefit? In real economic terms the cost would be minimal. If the new students learned something that was of subsequent value to themselves in work or leisure, or as citizens of a democratic society, there would be some economic return on the expenditure. Even if they spent a few years or months just enjoying themselves no harm would be done. Higher education would simply be another word for holiday. It would be a little bit unfair on those who, given the choice, would rather spend their enforced leisure playing (or watching) football or pinball but it might be argued by some that higher education even in purely recreational terms is of higher quality than these other activities.

However, this kind of argument takes an extremely simplistic view of both higher education and unemployment. Even if we are entering a period in which unemployment levels of five per cent and more will become the norm, unemployment will still remain a transitory state for most people.

Most of those who are unemployed will in some respects be actively looking for jobs and not anxious to commit themselves, even to courses of quite short duration, that will interfere with their chances of taking up a job that becomes available. Indeed, as soon as it starts to impede people from taking up productive employment, higher education would cease to be cost free in that it would begin to use the time of people that had alternative productive uses.

There will, of course, be a hard core of unemployed people who do eventually effectively give up actively looking for employment. The higher the overall level of unemployment the larger will be the hard core. However, the very characteristics that cause people to be at the end of the queue for jobs are also likely to make them the least able to benefit from higher education. The long-term unemployed are usually older, less well qualified and have lower levels of academic attainment and often less motivation than those in work. There are certainly education and training schemes that can, and ought, to be devised to help the long-term unemployed. But higher education, however liberally the term is interpreted, is not among them and neither are such schemes likely to be costless.

As has already become apparent from the variety of contributors to this volume, higher education for all means different things to different people and often a variety of things to the same person. This makes exercises in the economics of universal higher education difficult, since what is true of the costs and financing of three-year full-time courses for young people before they enter active life may well not be true of short, part-time post-experience courses disseminated mainly by radio and television.

Even if we adopt a more limited perspective, the concept of higher education for all can have a variety of meanings: it could mean higher education universally available on demand and largely paid for out of public funds[1]: it could mean higher education for all who can pay, in an appropriate variety of institutions; it could mean subsidized higher education for all who can pass certain entrance tests (which is more or less what we have at present); or it could mean a comprehensive system with different institutions linked in a single framework and arrangements for transfer of students between them. In academic discussion a certain vagueness is permissible: it helps to establish general principles. In real life, those who will be expected to pay for the new roles that 'higher education for all' implies, whether they be taxpayers (or their representatives in parliament) or employers, or fee-paying students, can be expected to want to know exactly what it is they are being asked to buy.

In the early 1970s 'universal' higher education seemed a natural enough progression from 'mass' higher education. It had come to have a quite precise definition in terms of the proportion of young people who continued their studies immediately or soon after leaving secondary school. Martin Trow (1974) whose perceptive analysis of mass higher education crystallized much of the sociological thinking about *mass* higher education in the 1960s wrote:

> Countries that develop a system of elite higher education in modern times seem able to expand it without changing its character in fundamental ways until it is providing places for about 15 per cent of the age group. At about that point the system begins to change its character; if the transition is made successfully the system is then able to develop institutions that can grow without being transformed till they reach about 50 per cent of the age group. Beyond that, and so far only in the United States, large sections of the population send nearly all their children to some form of higher education as it begins to move rapidly towards universal access.

Universal access in this passage clearly means a number between 50 per cent and 100 per cent of young people for a period of three to four years at the end of their teens and the first half of their twenties. The references to 'age group' and 'their children' makes this clear. The changes to which Trow refers are changes in the organization and content of courses necessary to cater for a much wider range of aptitudes and attitudes than was found when only the most academically inclined 10 per cent or less of a particular age group experienced higher education. He is making a valid point and at the same time offering a criterion which is admirably precise for anyone who may be concerned with a Policy Analysis and Review or programme-budgeting exercise to examine the costs of alternative forms of provision.

In 1977 about fifteen per cent of the eighteen to twenty-one year old age group in Britain were in some form of full-time higher education. At this level of provision about two per cent of Gross National Product and four per cent of public expenditure is devoted to higher education. If this fifteen per cent became sixty per cent and if we attempted to maintain existing staff-student ratios, relative salaries and methods of finance, we should need to allocate sixteen per cent of government expenditure to higher education. If universal higher education became really universal and accounted for 90 per cent of the age group we should need to devote 12 per cent of national income to higher education alone. At the same time expansion of secondary education would be necessary in order to support such enrolments in higher education so we may safely estimate

101

that universal higher education on the existing British model of staffing could come about only if at least 20 per cent of our total national income were devoted to secondary and higher education. These numbers would change little whether the prevalent pattern of provision was that of the universities, polytechnics, colleges of (higher) education or other forms of advanced further education. Such figures, even if they are wildly inaccurate, point clearly to the impossibility of achieving universal higher education on anything like the existing British pattern. Indeed, this was the point that Trow was making. Higher education in the United States and other countries where enrolment ratios are much higher than in Britain does not have the same intensity of economic input as in Britain. The ratio of staff to students is lower, student drop-out is higher and, in the United States at least, the average earnings of all academics relative to manual earnings is less. Even if it were desirable on educational grounds it is, therefore, not possible to envisage higher education for all in Britain as consisting simply of the expansion of existing institutions, whether the expansion occurs in universities, polytechnics or the more recent colleges and institutes of higher education. At the very least, staff student ratios would have to change and the relative economic position of the average teacher in higher education would almost certainly have to deteriorate.

Since the passage of Trow's was written, however, opinions about the way higher education is likely to develop in the future have changed considerably. In part under the pressure of stagnant, and sometimes declining, enrolments in such countries as the United States and Sweden, in part as a result of fears about the costs of untrammelled expansion of conventional higher education as in Germany and Holland, and in part because of an increasing realization in many countries that despite the great expansion of the 1960s higher education remains socially discriminatory, there has been a growing interest in 'lifelong education' as the pattern for future development of higher education. Lifelong education itself has many different patterns. To Clark Kerr and the Carnegie Commission in the United States it meant essentially 'two years in the bank', that is a procedure to enable young people to delay entry to post-secondary education without thereby depriving themselves entirely of the opportunity of higher education suited to their needs, interests and abilities. To the OECD it means recurrent education, that is the return to education by individuals at periods through their working lives. Recurrent education is often linked to the notion of 'paid educational leave' or 'sabbaticals for all', since if working people are to take advantage of educational opportunities, they and their dependents must have the means of maintaining their standards of living at somewhere near their previous levels. To the Council of Europe lifelong education has been associated with the idea of permanent education, that is individual adults making use of a whole variety of potential educational experience throughout their lives, such as radio and television, correspondence courses, magnetic tape and 'learning exchanges'.

What all these have in common, and where they all differ from the late 1960s view exemplified in the passage quoted, is that they envisage the upper reaches of education as being spread out in some way throughout the lifetime of individuals rather than concentrated before the beginning of their working lives. If higher education for all is to become a reality it is virtually certain that this is the sense in which it will do so. Courses of higher education must be within the reach of a much wider clientele than at present and must be accessible to people at all stages of their lives.

Cost considerations

A major difficulty in the economic appraisal of such schemes is that it is usually very difficult to pin them down to specific numbers and quantities in the way that Trow's scenario could be pinned down.

However, the general response of economists who have considered the issue is that the postponement of higher education for whatever reason is likely to prove more expensive than conventional higher education in relation to the benefits obtained. (See for example Blaug and Mace 1977, Simkins 1976, Stoikov 1975, Williams 1978.) In essence the two main economic problems are first that full-time education for adults is extremely expensive because of the high opportunity costs of earnings foregone, and secondly, that the later in life education is undertaken the smaller will be the rate of return on the investment in that education, because the individual will have a shorter period of life left in which to recoup the benefits. A possible third problem, which although psychological in origin has economic implications, is that, to the extent that older people find it harder than those who are younger to learn some subjects, it will be more expensive in terms of direct teaching inputs for them to achieve a given amount of educational gain. This last point is controversial and some of the evidence is contradictory. It is often claimed that adults with some work experience do better in some social science subjects for example than students straight from school. It is not, however, seriously disputed that ability to learn in adult life is powerfully influenced by educational experiences early in life. Those who have learned how to learn while young are able to carry on learning as adults much better than those whose early education was unsatisfactory.

One of the main difficulties in securing primary education for all in countries at early stages of economic development, is that there is substantial economic cost to families in giving up the income derived from their children's labour. In many of the industrial countries we still see the remains of this economic influence in the long summer holidays which were established, not so that families could go to the seaside, but so that children could help with the harvest.

As children get older the higher is the economic cost of their not being in productive employment. There is a fairly close association between the level of income of a country and the length of effective compulsory education for children. Legislation usually proves ineffective in the face of such economic pressures.

For adults the income foregone in any period of full-time education is normally much greater. If an individual is to bear these costs voluntarily himself he must anticipate substantial returns. The greater the income foregone, the greater the anticipated benefits need to be in order to make it worthwhile. Potential students of 'higher' education, however we define it, are likely to have the highest earnings to forego because in general they will also be the more successful members of the labour force. The later in life they seek higher education the greater in general will be their foregone earnings and the shorter will be the period of life left to recoup the returns on these costs. There are strong pressures on most individuals to push their higher education as early as possible in their lives if it conflicts in any way with their working lives (or indeed their family and social lives either).

One way of overcoming these pressures is to provide sufficient public subsidy to encourage people to do so. But what justification is there for seeking public funds for this purpose?[2]

One occurs where the public may be harmed by professional workers who do not update their skills. Medical practitioners who do not keep themselves informed about new developments may endanger their patients; lawyers who are not familiar with current legislation and judicial opinions may harm their clients' interests; teachers who give their pupils information that is wrong or who use teaching methods that are now known to be psychologically inappropriate can do considerable damage. In all such cases in the absence of legal compulsion which is impractical in most Western countries there is a clear case for some degree of public subsidy to encourage teachers, lawyers, doctors, engineers and others in similar positions to take advantage of new knowledge that becomes available.

Many current proposals aim at compelling employers to provide much of the requisite subsidy through awarding full pay during employees' periods of absence. Provision for paid educational leave is now enshrined in the legislation of several countries.

Benefits

Advocates of lifelong education for all quite understandably devote more attention to the benefits than to the costs. These benefits can be summarized as being concerned with personal development, with the promotion of social equality by ensuring that no-one is ever cut off from the opportunity to better himself through education, and with increasing productivity by offering workers frequent opportunities to update their skills and acquire new ones.

The nature of such benefits is that they accrue to people *after* a course of education. As already pointed out the older someone is when he undertakes a course of study the shorter the period of life left to him to enjoy the benefits. This is most obvious in the case of financial benefits of increased earnings but the principle is the same in any situation in which people give up some immediate gratification in order to obtain a flow of benefits afterwards. Such considerations clearly lead to a powerful criticism of any concept of mass lifelong education as an *alternative* to concentrating opportunities on younger people.

There are, however, two ways in which the force of such criticism is considerably reduced. The first is that where the education experience is *intrinsically* satisfying the 'sacrifice' of present gratification for future benefits is much reduced. This obviously needs to be borne in mind by adult educators. Secondly, the criticism is based on the belief that future benefits consist of a flow over the remainder of an individual's life. If, however, it is the case that many of these benefits are lost after a period of a few years then it is irrelevant from an economic viewpoint whether the investment in education occurs at the age of twenty or forty. If, as is often claimed for example, much of the knowledge gained in an engineering course is obsolete after ten years, the returns on investment in the training of forty year old engineers is potentially as great as those on twenty year old engineering students. Such considerations also offer an economic rationale for providing professional training to older women who have completed their child-bearing and wish to return to work (See Simkins 1977.).

It should be apparent by now that before any serious economic analysis of universal higher education can be undertaken several ambiguities need to be clarified. We can say with some degree of certainty that for economic reasons, and probably for others as well, the idea of a majority of the eighteen to twenty-one age group in some form of full-time higher education is not likely to be viable. In the United States which used to be considered the pioneer in higher education expansion a plateau in student numbers seems to have been reached in recent years.

We can also generalize fairly categorically that since the private and social opportunity costs of releasing adults for full-time courses of higher education are likely to be considerable, any viable system of widespread higher education opportunities must be based on part-time studies supplemented perhaps from time to time with short periods of intensive full-time study. Beyond that we can do little more than say that individual schemes need to be evaluated one by one.

The finance of higher education for all

In broad terms the finance for any type of education can be obtained either from the students or from other members of society. The rationale for arrangements for the first type is that, since individuals reap most of the benefits from their education, it is only fair that they should pay for it, either immediately or by borrowing and subsequently repaying the loan. The opposite case depends essentially on the view that society as a whole derives greater advantage from having its members educated than the individuals themselves benefit from their own education; in other words, that there are external benefits to society as a whole from the education of any individual. Since the kind of higher education provision being discussed in this book is likely to bring advantages both to individual students and to society as a whole there is clearly scope for a good deal of both empirical research and ideological debate for deciding the appropriate mix of financial sources.

The matter is complicated even more by arguments based on economic efficiency and on equity. If people have to pay for their own education some will get less education than is optimal, not because they do not want it but because they cannot afford it. Another problem is that even at the 'higher' levels, education is an activity where individuals are not well informed. As in medicine it is inevitable that many educational decisions must be made by professionals on behalf of, and in the interests of, people who are less expert. This implies a measure either of compulsion or of subsidy and in general the latter is considered more acceptable for adults.

Conversely if higher education is provided free, yet most of the benefits accrue to private individuals, there will be a tendency for the demand for it to be greater than economic efficiency (however defined) warrants. The problem is particularly acute if some of the claims about 'credentialism' are correct. Credentialism can be defined as occurring where people with higher education qualifications are preferred in the labour market even though nothing they can acquire in the course of their education warrants this preference. In this case there is a very serious danger that higher education for all would become simply an ever longer and eventually a lifelong scramble for qualifications with individuals obtaining advantage over their fellows at public expense.

Higher education *can* be offered as a purely commercial proposition and in some circumstances is. There was a flurry of interest in the mid-1970s in the United States in the private proprietary schools following the discovery by the Carnegie Commission that about eight per cent of the total enrolments in post-secondary education were in profit-making schools and that these were eligible for government subsidy.

In Britain there is little payment of fees for higher education although the initial success of the Independent University shows that in some circumstances fee-paying universities can establish themselves even in this country. Nor should it be forgotten that students at the Open University pay a substantial part of the costs of their courses.

However even if proprietary education is not acceptable as a pattern for the provision of universal higher education it does have some lessons for public sector establishments. It is utilitarian and flexible. Students paying the full costs of their courses are the customers and as in any commercial business the schools must satisfy their customers or lose their custom. So proprietary schools tend to be extremely accommodating to the needs of their students and there is greater flexibility over such matters as starting dates and lengths of courses.

As Peter Scott (1975) has pointed out:

The continuing vitality of proprietary education (in the United States) in the face of the massive expansion of Community Colleges has surprised many people. Community Colleges are cheap from the point of view of the student. They are usually modern and well equipped. They enjoy both the financial backing of the state and the blessing of the educator. They offer a balanced and rounded educational experience to their students. Yet the proprietary schools continue to thrive, and their success cannot be explained by the persistence of fast talking salesmen. They offer what many young people want, a vocational education that leads directly to a clear occupational goal in the shortest possible time. Accountability, and the flexibility that this implies, flow naturally from their need to show a profit. They aim to train, not to educate. At the same time, they provide an important service to young people that has too often been ignored by public colleges which have perhaps tried too hard and too consciously to educate their students whether they liked it or not.

Part Three: The Economic Implications

Of course, payment of fees by students and quasi-commercial operation of educational institutions is possible in the public sector also. There is, in Britain as in the United States, considerable willingness by large numbers of people to pay part of the direct costs of short courses and part-time courses provided they provide explicitly recognized recreational, cultural or vocational benefits. The clearest evidence of this in Britain is the massive success of evening classes, but there is a vast number of short full-time courses in adult education centres and universities and other colleges on subjects ranging from art appreciation to zoology. It is unlikely, however, that any system of higher education dependent on the payment of fees by private individuals can become genuinely universal.

If advantage is to be taken of the greater responsiveness of educational institutions to consumer wishes that finance by fees can bring, ways must be found of providing some degree of subsidy to the individuals paying the fees. The two most widely proposed sources of subsidy are the state and employers. In the next chapter Alan Maynard explores some of the issues in the public finance of higher education and they will not be rehearsed here. One proposal is, however, worth mentioning since it combines private and public financing in an interesting way. This is the scheme proposed by Gosta Rehn (1972) for an integrated educational, recreational and retirement fund.

In essence Rehn's proposal is that employees would pay contributions into a social insurance fund for educational and recreational purposes just as they already do for retirement pensions and in order to guarantee income in periods of sickness or unemployment. 'These educational costs, paid leave of absence (vacations or more extended sabbaticals) and retirement pensions would all be part of a single social insurance plan. Individuals would have relative freedom to select their lifetime patterns of non-work (e.g. more lifetime education and smaller retirement pension; short annual vacation and early retirement etc).' (Embling 1974). An aspect of the scheme which is interesting is the proposal that an individual should be allowed to draw from his *prospective* lifetime fund in order to finance periods of education early in his life or when it was particularly advantageous to him to do so. Analytically this is little different from proposals for loans which are discussed in the next chapter. Students would be borrowing money to pay fees against prospective future social insurance contributions.

However, the 'he who benefits should pay (somehow)' principle is not the only one possible in the public finance of higher education. A different principle is followed for the basic education of children and many people would argue should apply to higher education also. This is that every individual has the right to an education suited to his needs and that the State,

108

representing the collective interests of all individuals, has a responsibility to provide it. It is possible that by the end of the century it will be normal for adults to have a right to have their educational needs satisfied just as they can claim a right to have their medical needs met at the public expense.

There are, however, a number of difficulties in applying this principle to higher education for all. In the case of primary and secondary education, and to some extent in medicine, the potential demand for the service is fairly well bounded. Children need primary education during five or six years during which time all their non-educational costs can reasonably be met from their families (or non-educational subsidies). Similarly most people do not seek medical attention unless they are ill and the probability of being ill can be calculated actuarially with some degree of confidence. Even here, however, it is often claimed that unreasonable demands are made on free health services because patients have no knowledge of the real cost of the services they are receiving.

In open-ended higher education this difficulty is much greater. Some form of 'rationing' is likely to be necessary because educational potential of individuals is almost limitless and unless restraints are imposed some individuals may decide to devote their whole lives to realizing their full potential through education while others work and pay taxes in order to enable them to do so. If only a few people want, or are permitted to do this no practical difficulties arise and most societies have for centuries supported a tiny minority of the population in a life of scholarship or contemplation. Such a principle is not however viable in the context of higher education for all. There has to be some system for establishing priorities in allocating resources that is fair, efficient and not too costly.

This means either that individuals meet the costs of their own higher education albeit with the aid of financial mechanisms such as loans to ensure 'fairness' in the distribution of opportunities[3], or that administrative criteria must decide the terms on which courses should be available. If entry is limited by ability to pass examinations or (as in the case of the Open University) by externally perceived potential ability to pass examinations, this effectively limits provision to what is considered economically feasible. 'Higher education for all' implies that such hurdles do not exist, or at least that they are lowered to a level at which nearly everyone can jump them.

The economic dilemma and a solution

There is an underlying economic paradox facing protagonists of universal higher education. So long as not many people want it there are no practical economic problems, but it is not really higher education for all. As soon as it becomes popular some means has to be found of rationing it. The only realistic way of solving this paradox is through the reduction of costs. The one thing we can say with certainty is that higher education for all will have to be seen to be useful, enjoyable, and above all cheap. As with other mass consumption products from popular newspapers to popular wines there will be many in higher education who will claim that the masses are being made the subject of a confidence trick and that all the valuable qualities of the product are lost when it is mass-produced for the popular market. This views is wrong on at least two counts. 'Quality' products can continue to exist side by side with mass-consumed goods, the *Financial Times* alongside *The Sun*, 'Chateau Lafite' alongside 'Supermarket Red'. Indeed, quality is probably enhanced in the long run by the development of popular awareness. Secondly, there are good- and bad-quality cheap wines and newspapers and there can equally well be good- and bad-quality cheap higher education.

The aim of those who seriously wish to promote the cause of higher education for all must be to develop forms of higher education that are cheap but of good quality. The Open University appeared as if it was going to lead the way but there are increasing doubts about how far it is making full use of the cost saving or student number increasing potential of its educational technology. (See for example Laidlaw and Layard 1974, and Mace 1978.)

Polytechnics and further education colleges have some features of commodities produced for popular consumption but they too are developing along lines that are not cheap. They continue to have staffing ratios, levels of remuneration and conditions of work that may have been appropriate for higher education for a minority but which are certainly not feasible if it is to be open to all.

There are no insuperable economic problems in providing higher education of reasonable quality for all who want it throughout their lives. The difficulties in achieving it are mainly educational, social and political. Are we really willing to make the adaptations that are necessary in order to provide higher education for all? Higher education does have other functions as well as providing education and training facilities for students. There is a research and scholarship function to be performed as well. That this is not incompatible with mass higher education is illustrated by the United States, which country, as well as providing post-secondary education for a broader spectrum of students than any other, also dominates the Nobel prizes for science. What we need to develop in Britain – and in Europe generally – is an array of institutions (e.g. Brosan 1971) that complement each other, providing short courses of post-secondary vocational training at one end of the spectrum and post-doctoral research at the other. No single institution can undertake efficiently all these types of activities. On the other hard, no institution should be isolated financially, administratively or educationally from the rest of higher education. The first step in the establishment of higher education for all in Britain should be the abolition of the utterly wasteful binary system.

Notes

[1] A problem here is that it would lead to far too unrestricted training for professions like medicine and law, which would get far too many entrants. The situation in Italy which opened the doors of all its universities to all comers in 1969 should act as a cautionary tale to anyone thinking along these lines.

[2] By focusing on higher or post-secondary education we eliminate one justification for public subsidy, the remedying of obvious social disabilities such as illiteracy etc.

[3] The argument that some people are (and for some reason are likely to remain) too poor for the loan-type solution to be realistic is met by the reply that of course it is in order for society to subsidize its poorest members. But this is most equitably done by subsidization of income generally rather than earmarked subsidies for special purposes.

Bibliography

BLAUG, M. and MACE, J. (1977), Recurrent Education: The New Jerusalem. *Higher Education*, vol. 6, no. 3 August.

BROSAN, G. (1971), *Patterns and Policies (for Higher Education)*, Penguin.

EMBLING, J. (1974), *A Fresh Look at Higher Education*, Elsevier.

LAIDLAW, B. and LAYARD, R. (1974), Traditional versus Open University Teaching Methods: A Cost Comparison. *Higher Education*, vol. 3, no. 4, Nov.

MACE, J. (1978) Mythology in the Making: Is the Open University really Cost-effective. *Higher Education* vol. 7, no. 4.

REHN, G. (1972), 'Prospective View on Patterns of Working Time' in *Report of International Conference on New Patterns of Working Time* OECD, Paris.

STOIKOV, V. (1975), *The Economics of Recurrent Education and Training*. International Labour Office, Geneva.

SIMKINS, T. (1976), Recurrent Education: Some Economic Issues. *Higher Education*, vol. 5, no. 4, Nov.

SCOTT, P. (1975), *Strategies of Post-Secondary Education*. Croom-Helm.

TROW, M. (1974), 'Problems in the Transition from Elite to Mass Higher Education' in *Policies for Higher Education*, OECD, Paris.

WILLIAMS, G.L. (1978). *Towards Higher Education: A new Role for Higher Education Institutions*, UNESCO.

7. Economic Aspects of State Intervention

Alan Maynard

Introduction

The purpose of this paper is to critically appraise the idea of universal higher education from the economic point of view. The first section is concerned with the definition and a brief analysis of some of the problems of the concept of universal higher education. In the second section the economic rationale of government involvement in the finance and provision of the service is examined. Despite the conclusion that the case for such government involvement is weak, it is argued in section three, that because of imperfections in the political decision-making process, State intervention will increase. This outcome may be unfortunate from the point of view of the efficient allocation of resources but the degree of misallocation can be mitigated if the education industry is prepared in greater measure to pursue more effective assessment of its internal workings. The methods by which efficiency might be increased are discussed in section four. The final section summarizes the main arguments in the paper.

What is universal higher education?

Education is a process by which people acquire skills and have their tastes and preferences changed through their life-cycle. A dictionary would have us believe that this process is systematic but for many people it is a haphazard process which takes place in the home, in the school, in the college and the university, on the job, in church, in the armed forces, via television and other media, by self-education, and by learning from experience. The education profession is wont to take a very blinkered view of the education process and, in doing so, perhaps exaggerate the importance of its contribution. The economist takes a more comprehensive view of education and regards it as a life-cycle process of investment and consumption by the household. The investment aspects of education endow individuals with skills or knowledge which affect the future productivity of the human being and generate increased future earnings flows. The consumption aspects of education give satisfaction in the present time period and do not affect lifetime earnings.

112

At present about fifteen per cent of the eighteen to twenty-one year old age groups are involved in one form or another of higher education. The proposals to make higher education universal have not been clearly articulated. At one extreme they could mean that all members of the eighteen to twenty-one year old age group have the right to higher education. This would seem to be a definition with little sense, not the least because most people do not even have education in the sixteen to eighteen year old age range. A more moderate definition of the term might follow from Trow (1974) who seems to argue that universal higher education involves fifty to one hundred per cent of young people in the eighteen plus age group having access to education for a period of three to four years. Why only this younger age group? Why three or four years?

The logic of this policy is not clear. To increase the entry into some university faculties could have explosive policy implications even if the costs of the education itself could be met. In France, West Germany, Italy and Belgium, where the easing of entry restrictions into medical schools took place in the late 1960s, the number of 'trained' doctors has increased and augments doctor stocks which are already high (Maynard and Walker 1978). In medicine supply tends to create its own demand and the financial implications of an increased supply of doctors has been rapid increases in expenditure on health care. Clearly the intake into some subjects would have to be carefully controlled unless it is possible to persuade such professionals to accept lower levels of remuneration.

If the supply of skilled manpower is increased and its rate of reward declines relatively through time, the rate of return to investing in increased supplies of skill will decline. The rate of return to investment in human capital is obtained by analysing the time discounted costs of education; this can be done separately for the individual who is doing the investing (in which case the major opportunity cost in the United Kingdom is earnings foregone during the training process), or for society as a whole (earnings foregone and the costs of education which are borne by the taxpayer), and the time discounted benefits thereof (expressed in terms of a proportion (usually about sixty per cent) of increased earnings throughout the life cycle. (See Blaug 1970). The application of this technique to education in the United Kingdom has shown that the rate of return to society of many types of education is low and in some cases negative, i.e. the costs exceed the benefits. By subsidizing students, the private cost of education is reduced, the private rate of return is raised above the social rate and students are induced to consume more education. Even so the rates of return, whether private or social, are low and it is clear that investment in most types of education is an inefficient way to spend resources. Society can get better

113

returns from investment elsewhere.

The implication of this for any policy of universal higher education is clear. The rates of return, private and social, to investment in higher education are low. Increased supplies of such educated people will depress the rate of return still more because the conventional predicted effect of such a flow would be that firstly the earnings of those so educated might be depressed, and secondly the earnings of those not so educated would rise because of their decreased numbers, greater scarcity and hence greater remuneration (hence the educateds' foregone earnings would rise).

An alternative view of universal higher education could be that it is consumption rather than investment. The proponents of this view would recognize the existence of the low rate of return to investment in higher education and would argue that higher education is consumption, that is it gives returns in the present period. Higher education in this case is a form of disguised unemployment. A critic of this view of the world might ask why we should be concerned with the consumption of higher education when our concern for other consumption acts, for instance the consumption of cars, colour televisions, cabbages and apple pies, is minimal? Is higher education 'special' or are the education professionals and policy-makers concerned with the wasteful use of scarce economic resources?

This brief examination of the definition of universal higher education has indicated that the available definitions are ambiguous and the logic of a policy of universal higher education (however defined) is not clear. Within the space constraints of this paper it has not been possible to discuss fully the extent of all these problems. However one problem which deserves more extensive examination is the subject of the next section.

Why should the state be involved in the finance and provision of higher education?

Whether higher education is universal or selective, careful consideration has to be given to the logic of government intervention in the provision and finance of higher education. Why can't individuals be left to pursue their goals without government interference? Why might such market outcomes be inefficient?

The first problem of the market which is alleged to exist by its critics is that the price system does not take account of all the relevant costs and benefits which are necessary to inform efficient decision-makers. This externality argument takes a variety of forms. Its essence is that market prices take account only of private benefits (increased remuneration over the life-cycle in the case of education) and ignore the benefits of higher education which accrue to society.

What are the social benefits of higher education? These benefits are usually poorly articulated and rarely measured. Arguments such as a more highly-educated society will be more civilized and conducive to economic growth are ambiguous and lack substantive evidence. Whether the more highly-educated are more or less deviant, or more or less prepared to oppose the social changes occasioned by economic growth, is debatable! Some might argue that the more highly-educated have different patterns of deviance and oppose economic growth because it threatens to make their skills redundant because of the process of technological change inherent in the growth process. However, the woolliness of these arguments does not inhibit even those opposed to them (e.g. Crew and Young 1977) to conclude that because of this type of market 'failure', individuals should be subsidized in the hope that this will encourage them to consume the socially efficient level of higher education.

In all cases it is argued that the externalities arise from the consumption of education. The implication is that greater consumption by groups which under-consume in the market, would rectify the market 'failure'. Firstly it is important to note that this argument, if accepted, implies only that there is a need for government financial involvement. By augmenting incomes the private individual can be persuaded by government subsidies to increase his consumption to the efficient level. Government provision of education is sensible only if it is more efficiently produced than the private market output.

Secondly the argument is that the externality arises from consumption of education. This argument is rather peculiar for it manifests a concern about inputs (i.e. the level of resources going into education) rather than about outcomes. I would argue that externalities in education arise not from differences in consumption but from differences in the level of final outcome, 'education' itself. This distinction is important because it focuses attention on the need to measure outcomes and discuss education policy outcomes and their relationship, if any, with education inputs. Consumption of education inputs (e.g. the services of teachers) may have little effect on the outcome of the education process. Concentration of attention on this distinction between ends (educational outcomes) and means (education inputs or policy) indicates that the discussion of externalities has been inadequate, blurred the distinction between ends and means, and offered no substantive case for State involvement in education.

A second argument put forward by the proponents of State involvement in higher education is that individuals are not as fully informed about the relative benefits of higher education as they should be. This argument is fraught with difficulties. Firstly it is not clear what is the efficient level of information about the relative attributes of higher education and other activities. Information, like beer, is a scarce commodity whose supply can be increased only by foregoing other goods and services.

Secondly it can be argued that the supply of information is inhibited by the nature of the education markets' structure which gives considerable powers to professional groups who have little incentive to behave in an efficient manner. Whilst there might be disagreement about some of Illich's views (Illich *et al.* 1977) the economic literature on the professions (Maynard 1978) seems to lend some force to his arguments that they are not always institutions which encourage the efficient use of resources and the generation of efficient levels of information about higher education, outcomes and input combinations.

The discussion of information problems leads to some interesting value judgements. Such behaviour is inherent in many of the utterances of the education profession who claim that students are unable to make choices efficiently because they cannot perceive the merits of alternative courses and modes of teaching. Whether the professionals have much hard evidence about the relative merits of alternative courses and alternative modes of teaching is very doubtful. Any attempt to answer it by studying the literature leads one to be highly sceptical of the ability of the professional to know better than his student, the attributes of courses. For the professional to claim expertise where he does not appear to have it is sad enough, but then for him to claim that he can make choices more efficiently than students, seems to be bold at best and silly at worst. The foundations of paternalism often tend to be built on the quicksands of ignorance and education seems to be no exception.

A third set of arguments favoured by those advocating government involvement in the higher education market seems to be bound up with distributional considerations. The argument seems to be that access to the higher education market is unequal, this outcome is unsatisfactory, and access should be made more equitable. This type of argument is concerned with the rules under which higher education is to be distributed. It is not concerned with the nature of the product, only with who is to get it. With income and wealth distributed unevenly, access to higher education is unequal. However before considering the mechanisms by which resources can be equalized to attain a more equal distribution of education, it is necessary to consider the rules under which they could be used to a allocate resources.

The first principle which could be used is that of justice. This idea of justice as fairness has been discussed a great deal recently as a result of

Rawls' book (Rawls 1972). For Rawls, equality is not a uniquely justifying concept. It is part of justice and will be achieved if justice is achieved. The Rawlsian argument asks for people who do not know their role or position in society to choose, from behind a veil of ignorance, a set of principles of fairness for the distribution of any good or service. It is difficult to see how the people behind the veil of ignorance can choose if they are ignorant of the workings of society.

This choice mechanism leads to the evolution of the principle that an uneven distribution is just if, and only if, it is to the advantage of the least well-endowed members of society. This principle of difference when applied to education means that anyone can have more education only if it is to the advantage of the less well-educated. For instance the greater education of a group of consultant physicians might be to the advantage of the less well-educated groups in society if they benefit from the health care services provided by these consultants. However the problems with the Rawlsian difference principle are numerous and centre around the ambiguity of the concept, Rawls' use of words, and whether society wishes to use the difference principle as the sole criterion for choice. These problems are nicely summarized by Warnock (1977) and need detain us no longer here.

Warnock discusses two other principles of distribution, that of compassion and that of envy. The compassion principle is a paternalistic concern for the needs of less well-endowed groups. Warnock cites Crosland (1962) and Tawney (1931) in her discussion of this but an equally interesting set of literature is that centred round health care (Culyer 1976). With this principle higher education would be distributed according to need as defined by some group. Obviously there are differing definitions of need and unless criteria are constructed to define and measure need, this set of arguments can be modified to justify any distribution.

Nozick's principle of envy, 'the envious man prefers neither one having it (in our case higher education) to others having it and he not having it', leads to the conclusion that if you prefer equality it is best that neither of two people have higher education, than that any one person should have it. This seems to be an argument in favour of universality or no provision of higher education. Rather than have some but not all in the higher education system, the bene-olent despotic decision-maker prefers to have no-one consuming such education or everyone consuming. The reason for this in the Nozick-type world is that the despot dislikes the notion of success or failure.

Either no-one should succeed or fail, or all should have access to higher education and all will be deemed successes by the reformation of existing procedures. This notion of equality may be inefficient because it destroys

Part Three: The Economic Implications

the process of selection or filtering inherent in the education process.

The equity criteria suggested by Rawls and others are incomplete. No clear rules for distributing education seem to be available at this level of discussion. This unsatisfactory outcome leads to the conclusion that it is not clear how resources or access to higher education should be distributed. Maybe it is best to leave individual decision-makers to allocate their resources privately rather than with State intervention.

Whether the reader agrees with this conclusion or not, the financial problems of the higher education market could be rectified with student grants and State subsidization of education being replaced by a different system of finance.

Several generations of students have now had access to a generous system of financial support for higher education in the United Kingdom. It is interesting to examine the effects of such arrangements on the socio-economic composition of the population in higher education. An analysis of the data on the socio-economic characteristics of the population of universities indicates that the present system of grants has had relatively little effect on the progression of working-class children entering university degree courses. The Robbins Report (1963) surveyed the evidence for the period 1928 to 1961 and showed that, although female working-class participation had increased, the total participation rate for the group was static.

Table 1. University Applications 1974 (percentages)

Occupation group of parent	Accepted	Not accepted	Total	Census 1971 (Males 45–59)
Miners and quarrymen	0·6	0·6	0·6	2·4
Engineering and allied trades workers	7·2	8·5	7·8	15·3
Labourers	1·2	1·5	1·4	7·2
Clerical workers	11·5	10·7	11·1	7·0
Administrators and managers	15·2	14·2	14·8	7·2
Professional, technical workers, artists	34·1	29·8	32·1	9·3

Source: Universities Central Council on Admissions, Statistical Report to the Twelth Report 197304, Cheltenham, 1975 table E1, page 11.

Table 1 shows some more recent data. The table shows the occupation groups of parents of U.K. University applicants in 1974 and the number of males aged forty-five to fifty-nine years of age in that occupation group in 1971 (the nearest census year). The labourer category makes up 7·2 per cent of males in the forty-five to fifty-nine age groups in the 1971 census. The percentage of all applicants whose parent was a labourer in

1974 was 1·4. Thus applicants from the labourer category were 'under-represented' by 5·8 percentage points. Also it can be seen that the acceptance rates for these applicants is relatively low. On the other hand the children of professional, technical workers and artists were over-represented. Only 9·3 of the work force were in this category in 1971 but over 34 per cent of those accepted for places in universities came from this class. As the Robbins Report noted many years ago, the percentage of children coming to universities from working-class backgrounds has been relatively static since the 1920s. Most of the expansion of the university system has benefited people who come from relatively affluent backgrounds. Why we should be prepared to redistribute resources to people coming from relatively privileged backgrounds and who, in terms of life-time income, may be affluent, is a question which is seldom asked and usually answered by the emotive pressure-group responses of those who benefit from the present system of financial support.

The present system of government financial support for higher education appears to redistribute resources to the offspring of middle-income households. I do not favour subsidizing those who may be potentially affluent in terms of life-time earnings, but who are temporarily poor. The temporary poverty of the student groups results from their lack of earning power because of their involvement in the education process and their lack of collateral which makes it difficult for them to borrow. The capital market will not lend if there is no security for a loan. The student is investing in herself and with increased life-time earning flows could pay off her debt. Unfortunately the student may, for instance, migrate and avoid debt repayment. The capital market has failed to evolve institutions to overcome this in most cases. An exception is the Cranfield MBA course where banks lend to students and Cranfield offers security by guaranteeing repayment.

Emulation of the Cranfield example by, for instance, the State guaranteeing loan repayment to banks, could give students access to a means of finance for their studies. If the State could identify and quantify relevant externalities it could also subsidize such loans to ensure the efficient level of investment in higher education. Similarly if the State wished to advantage some socio-economic groups (e.g. the working class) or other identifiable groups (e.g. females and coloureds), it could subsidize loans to these groups. The student loan policy is potentially more flexible and efficient than the present financial arrangements for higher education. It offers the possibility of subsidizing particular groups, clearly identifying the costs of such aid, and enabling those able to pay for their education in later life, to finance their education by a loan.

An alternative to the loans system is the scheme proposed by Rehn (OECD 1972) and mentioned by Gareth Williams in the preceding chapter.

119

This scheme proposes the integration of the retirement, recreational and educational programmes into one scheme. Employees would pay contributions to a fund which would finance the recreational, the retirement and the educational aspect of the life cycle after leaving school. Thus the individual would pay contributions and as a result get a pension and finance for his education and recreation. Several problems are inherent in this idea. Is the plan concerned solely with the redistribution of an individual's resources throughout his life cycle? Or is it concerned with redistributing resources between fund members? Or is it concerned with both aspects? The objectives of the scheme need to be clearly articulated. If membership of the scheme is compulsory the rationale of such compulsion is not readily evident. If individuals had wanted such benefits they could have bought them on the private insurance market. Obviously private schemes would not generally offer the possibility of borrowing to finance education at eighteen years of age which was financed out of later insurance contributions. However it is apparent that some forms of the Rehn scheme might well be loan schemes in disguise. Whether it is more efficient to finance higher education through a loans scheme or by using a variant of the Rehn proposal is an empirical question, which cannot be answered in the absence of careful monitoring of experiments with the alternative mechanisms.

This section has examined the economic rationale of government intervention on higher education and found it wanting. The externality argument is weak and fraught with difficulties which have been poorly articulated and badly analysed. The ignorance of the consumer/lack of information argument is also inadequate in that it fails to indicate how the efficient level of information can be identified and ignores the power of the education profession as an agent for reducing information in education markets. The argument about the distribution of income and access to finance offers no widely acceptable set of rules with which redistributive policy can be guided and appears to indicate that a system of student loans might be more efficient than the present arrangements. These arguments are not novel (Maynard 1975). Yet they are fundamental in the sense that they question the foundations of present policies. Why have these arguments had so little impact on the formation of education policy in the United Kingdom? An attempt to shed some light on this question is the concern of the next section.

The inevitable growth of higher education

In the previous section I have argued that the economic rationale of government intervention in higher education is defective. Despite this conclusion it is likely that the role of government in higher education will increase. The purpose of this section is to try to explain why this outcome may be produced. The explanation is concerned with the economic analysis of the professions, bureaucracy and political behaviour.

The objectives of licensed professions are unclear. On the one hand the members of the professions claim that their organizations are in the 'public interest'. As I have argued in another context (Maynard 1978) the public interest argument is often weak when subjected to close analysis. Most of the public interest arguments are bound up with the belief that the individual is not the best judge of his own welfare. The argument is that the supply of information about the efficiency of education is inadequate and that the 'expert' professional is the best decision-maker. Only those with the requisite skills are licensed to practise in the profession and the licence protects the individual and society from market imperfections in information and decision-making ability.

As I have argued above, these contentions are ambiguous. Some of the arguments are differences in value judgements and cannot be refuted by evidence. Those arguments that can be tested have not been examined closely and the circumstantial evidence that is available would tend to make most observers wary of the argument's validity.

If the licensing of the professions is not in the public interest an alternative rationale of its existence is that it is in the interests of the profession. Stigler (1971) has argued that professional bodies seek, acquire, design and operate State regulation primarily for the benefit of those who are regulated; self-interest is the driving force behind regulation. Moore (1961) deployed a similar set of arguments. The essence of these arguments is that the profession can protect and further its pecuniary and non-pecuniary interests by getting the State to regulate its activities and by ensuring that the regulated control the regulators.

Thus the argument is that professionals (be they members of any of the teachers' unions – NUT, AUT, NATFHE etc.) seek regulation to further their interests by increasing their life-time earnings, improving job tenure and ensuring increased expenditure by government in their sector. This pressure may not be rejected by bureaucrats and politicians.

Following Niskanen (1973) a plausible objective of bureaucrats is that they seek to maximize their budgets. Niskanen argues that a criterion for promotion in bureaucracies is the rate of growth of the bureau's budget. The 'successful' bureaucrat is one whose budget increases over time. This simple hypothesis has been debated at length and offers some interesting insights into bureaucratic behaviour. The civil servant may wish to see his bureau or department grow because of the effects of growth on his career prospects. The professional may see the bureaucrat as his ally. If the bureaucrat is successful, his increased budget will be used to buy more of the professional's services. Consequently following Stigler and Niskanen, it is not unusual to see the regulated closely co-operating with and 'guiding' the regulator. The professional, to varying extents, can generate the demand for his services.

Will the politicians countervail the pressures of the bureaucrats and the professionals? In the political market place politicians provide policies which induce voters to remain loyal to them or switch their votes to them. The Downsian model (Downs 1957) assumes that the politician is concerned with maximizing his satisfaction from life and the thing which generates satisfaction for him is the acquisition and maintenance of political power. In the Downsian world the out-of-office politician offers policies which will 'buy' him votes and enable him to acquire power. The in-office politician will offer policies which compete with his rivals but which have the same objective: maintenance and acquisition of votes.

The Downsian vote-maximization hypothesis has been amplified by Tullock (1976) who has argued that on any coalition of voters, the median voter tends to be crucial in any system of choice with majority voting. If we have a three-person world (A, B and C) and three alternative higher education policies: 15 per cent of the age group in higher education (policy 1), 50 per cent of the age group in higher education (policy 2), and 85 per cent of the age group in higher education (policy 3); with A preferring policy 1, B preferring policy 2, and C preferring policy 3, the policy outcome is likely to be 2. Individual A prefers policy 1 but he also prefers policy 2 to policy 3 because it is nearer to 1. Individual B prefers policy 2 and is indifferent between policies 1 and 3. Individual 3 prefers policy 3 but he also prefers policy 2 to policy 1 as it is nearer to 3. The likely outcome is policy 2, the first preference of B (the median voter) and the second preference of A and C. This simple median voter theorem has been proved to have relatively good predictive powers. The analysis indicates that the politician in an attempt to gain or retain office must sell policies which appeal to the median voter. The politician is not concerned with the 'public interest' but with his tenure of office.

The implications of this analysis for higher education are profound. One result of the Tullock analysis is that the outcomes of the political process may favour the middle-class (median) income groups. Social policy may entail redistribution to the middle classes, as happens now with university student support. Furthermore the professions by using their persuasive powers and prestige as the 'expert' group, may be able to augment the demand for its services. The profession tends to be predominant in giving policy advice, the bureaucrats favour the expansion of their empires and the politicians are unwilling and/or incapable of countervailing these forces because of the electoral effects, in terms of votes, of their behaviour. The education industry is very labour intensive and carries within it many votes.

This pessimistic scenario is arrived at by generalizing and simplifying the analysis of many contributors to the theory of political economy. The argument is that because of the nature of our political and social institutions the combined effects of professional groups, bureaucrats, and the politicians is such that there is an inexorable drive for budget expansion despite the evidence that the effects of the present education system in terms of efficiency and equity objectives are poor. Unless the institutions change we will have to spend resources unwisely and illogically. How can the institutions be changed?

Towards a more efficient education system

The existing system of financing and providing higher education provides little incentive for decision-makers to pursue more efficient behaviour patterns. What incentives are there for an academic to be a good teacher? What incentives are there for an academic to be a good researcher? Do academics make good administrators? Academics have to perform all three functions, teaching, researching and administrating, to greater or lesser degrees. Why don't they specialize in particular functions? What do we know about their efficiency in carrying out these functions?

One set of standard responses to such questions is to query the sanity of the writer and/or argue that you cannot measure the characteristics of the education process. The latter sentiments are deplorable and merely examples of where 'academic freedom' and restrictive practices may be at one. Obviously there are difficulties in measuring the performance of the education system but it is possible to measure the effects (or lack of them!) of the teaching process. For instance what do we know about the efficiency of economics teaching in British universities? Might it not be more efficient to have one national set of televised first-year lectures backed up by tutorials, careful monitoring of effectiveness and the more widespread use of teaching machines? The Esmée Fairbairn Economics Research Centre at Heriot-Watt University has been attempting to carry out a systematic appraisal of our activities in recent years. This research followed on from Lumsden's (1974) work in the United States which showed the virtues (in terms of a variety of performance indicators) of programmed learning. The lessons of this research have not affected practice much: the technology remains the same as that deployed by the Greeks of old – chalk and talk. Although we know little about the costs and outputs of universities we have even less systematic evidence about the performance of polytechnics and colleges of education. As in the case of universities, the analysis of the performance of colleges and polytechnics is difficult. However with the noble exception of Verry and Davies' study (1976) and a few others, the desire to ask questions, let alone attempt to provide answers, about the cost effectiveness of teaching techniques and the optimum sizes of universities, colleges, polytechnics and departments therein, is noticeable by its absence. Society continues to be happy to spend resources with little systematic monitoring of the efficiency of resource allocation in higher education.

The efficiency of resource allocation outside the State education sector system in industrial training is equally questionable. The magnitude of the sums spent on industrial training are often overlooked. Maureen Woodhall, after examining the inadequate statistics, gives a U.K. industrial training expenditure figure of around £1000 million in 1971 (Woodhall and Vernon 1972). As Woodhall notes, this figure is little more than a guess, but clearly much more is spent on industrial training than on, for instance, the universities (£408 million in 1972–3). Little is known about the efficiency with which this vast sum is spent. Prior to the Industrial Training Act (1962) the quality of training was criticized as often being little more than 'sitting with Nellie'. Since 1962 there is a belief that the quality of training has improved but there is little systematic information available to substantiate this hypothesis. The Department of Employment estimates that at any one time about 1,200,000 people are receiving training of one sort and another. It seems that we can only guess at the cost of this training and have little idea of its quality. Similarly we have little idea who benefits from this training expenditure and so it is impossible to even guess about the distribution of the benefits of industrial training.

Around 1971–2 as much as £1400 million may have been spent on the finance of industrial training and universities in the United Kingdom. If account is taken of other types of formal education and other labour market expenditures it is clear that well in excess of £2000 million was being spent on the training and education of people over the age of 16. The reason why it is difficult to acquire more recent data for items such as industrial training is that whilst the State is encouraging expenditure by Industrial Training Boards and firms, no data is collected on a regular basis to assess how much training is carried out or how efficiently it is provided. Whilst more recent data on the quantity of resources used by the State education sector is available, there is little evidence about quality, or the efficiency of resource utilization and much evidence of significant inequalities in the distribution of benefits.

This inefficient behaviour with regard to resource utilization is clearly deplorable. Despite the evidence that decision-making behaviour is inefficient the education profession has shown great unwillingness to develop incentive systems which could lead to the adoption of more effective techniques. This unwillingness could be interpreted as another example of the pursuit of self-interested policies by the profession rather than the pursuit of policies conducive to the attainment of efficient outcomes. The licensing of the profession appears to have offered inadequate incentives for the pursuit of 'good practice' and, in some cases, appears to have inhibited the attainment of such a goal.

The adoption of mechanisms such as differential remuneration systems, new budgeting systems, peer review and education audit could, by changing monetary and non-monetary incentives, encourage practitioners to pursue more effective procedures. Differential remuneration systems could, by generating appropriate financial rewards, give practitioners incentives to adopt particular techniques, or work in particular subject or geographical areas. If there is a shortage of mathematicians why not pay them more than historians or sociologists? The efficiency of such techniques is not clear but their potential is attractive and needs to be tested rigorously in carefully monitored and controlled experiments.

New budgeting systems would seem also to be potentially very productive as a means of inducing a more effective use of education resources. The variety of potential schemes is enormous. Departmental management teams could be given a budget with which to employ staff (all types) and hire capital equipment. The opportunity cost of particular inputs would then be made clear to the decision-maker by providing a set of shadow prices and he would have the ability to experiment with differing input combinations. The members of the teams could be given ownership of residual monies at the end of each budgetary period.

Peer review, a mechanism by which peers or equals can monitor and influence the behaviour of individual decision-makers, or education audit, a mechanism by which an outside third party can monitor and influence the behaviour of individual educationalists, are both mechanisms worthy of careful study. In medicine peer review appears to be more effective in reducing deviance from group norms when the groupings are small. As the group size increases, deviant behaviour (in relation to the group norm of 'good practice') may reassert itself. In all cases of peer review the initial definition of 'good practice' is important and the effectiveness of the review is highly sensitive to this definition.

The education audit system would establish the right of a third party to monitor and influence the behaviour of educators. The audit, if effective, would reduce deviance from the externally determined group norm. There are some obvious problems with such a mechanism. Firstly it is difficult to identify 'qualified' third parties who are competent to determine norms. Lack of technical expertise may induce the third party to establish conservative norms which have only minor effects on practice. Another problem with the audit mechanism is that the auditor can control only relative costs, i.e. the costs of one educationalist *vis-à-vis* another. If absolute cost norms are not effectively established, the auditor may control relative costs but leave absolute costs unaffected.

The incentive to develop these mechanisms is limited. However the more extensive use of these incentive systems is essential if more effective use of resources is to be attained. In the field of medical care where the same problems exist, incentive mechanisms are being developed and implemented at a rate which clearly indicates the backwardness of the education profession. Both professions are reluctant to change their ways but change is being and will be forced on them by growing public awareness of the lack of accountability in higher education and the behaviour of enlightened mavericks who believe that there is great scope for attaining increased efficiency in resource allocation at all levels of the education process.

Summary

In section one some definitions of universal higher education were analysed and some of the inherent problems of the alternative definitions were examined. In the second section the rationale of government intervention in higher education was critically appraised. The arguments were found generally to be ambiguous, value laden and inadequate. A rational alternative policy to that pursued at present would seem to be a system of student loans. Despite the lack of substance in the case for government involvement in higher education, it was argued in section three that government involvement would increase because it served the interests of the education profession, bureaucrats and vote-maximizing politicians. The final substantive section, four, is concerned with the development of incentive mechanisms whereby the efficiency of resource allocation can be improved. The introduction of such mechanisms into all levels of education is tardy but will be encouraged by the behaviour of innovating maverick educators and the public realization of the lack of substantive scrutiny of expenditure on education.

Despite the evidence that higher education has little effect in terms of life-time income and despite the evidence that the effects of the education process are perhaps quite small (Jencks 1975, Taubman 1974, Atkinson

1975), the education profession works to maintain the view that its product is important. The case in favour of extending the size of the higher education sector is in need of clearer articulation. At present it is lacking. Even if there is a good case for such a policy the resources to finance it should come not from increments in expenditure but from the freeing of resources by the more effective use of the present budget. There is a need for the careful analysis of policy objectives, for the creation of incentives to pursue efficient allocation policies, and for a more careful and analytical approach to proposals to extend the size of the population having access to higher education.

Bibliography

ATKINSON, A.B. (1975), *The Economics of Inequality*, Oxford University Press, Oxford and London.

BLAUG M. (1970), *An Introduction to the Economics of Education*, Penguin, London.

CREW M.A. and YOUNG A. (1977), *Paying by Degrees*, Institute of Economic Affairs, London.

CROSLAND A. J. (1962), *The Conservative Enemy*, Jonathan Cape, London.

CULYER A. J. (1976), *Need and the National Health Service*, Martin Robertson, London.

DOWNS A. (1957), *An Economic Theory of Democracy*, Harper and Row, London and New York.

ILLICH I., ZOLA I.K., McKNIGHT J., CAPLAN J. and SHAIKEN H. (1977), *Disabling Professions*, Marion Boyars, London.

JENCKS C. (1975), *Inequality*, Penguin, London.

LUMSDEN K.G. (ed.) (1974), *Efficiency in Universities: the La Paz Papers*, Elsevier, Amsterdam.

MAYNARD A. (1975), *Health Care in the European Community*, Croom Helm, London.

MAYNARD A. (1978), 'The Medical Profession and the Efficiency and Equity of Medical Care', *Social and Economic Administration*, vol. 12, no. 1.

MAYNARD A. and WALKER A. (1978), 'Medical Manpower Planning in Three West European Countries', unpublished mimeograph.

MOORE J.G. (1961), 'The Purpose of Licensing', *Journal of Law and Economics*, vol. 4.

NISKANEN W. (1973), *Bureaucracy: Servant or Master*, Institute of Economic Affairs, London.

NOZICK A.R. (1974), *Anarchy, State and Utopia*, Basic Book and Blackwells.

OECD (Organisation for Economic Co-operation and Development) (1972), 'Prospective View of Patterns of Working Time' in *Report of the International Conference on New Patterns of Working Time*, Paris

RAWLS J. (1972), *Theory of Justice*, Oxford University Press, Oxford and London.

ROBBINS REPORT (1963), *Report of the Committee on Higher Education*, Cmnd. 2154, HMSO London.

STIGLER G. (1971), 'The Theory of Regulation', *Bell Journal of Economics and Management Science*, vol. 2, no. 1.

TAUBMAN P. (1974), *The Sources of Inequality*, North Holland, Amsterdam.

TAWNEY R.H. (1931), *Equality*, Unwin, London.

TROW M. (1974), 'Problems in the Transition from Elite to Mass Higher Education', in *Policies for Higher Education*, Organisation for Economic Co-operation and Development, Paris.

Part Three: The Economic Implications

TULLOCK G. (1976), *The Vote Motive*, Institute of Economic Affairs, London.
VERRY D. and DAVIES B. (1976), *University Costs and Outputs*, Elsevier, Amsterdam.
WARNOCK M. (1977), *Schools of Thought*, Faber, London.
WOODHALL, M. and WARD, V. (1972) *Economic Aspects of Education*, NFER, Slough.

PART FOUR

The Political Implications

8. A Conservative View

Keith Hampson

Debates about the function of higher education, the balance of subjects and the question of numbers, have occurred throughout history, and reveal the pre-occupations of society at a particular moment. Harold Macmillan always felt that having a historical perspective was salutary for a politician. But in British educational planning we seem to be unaware of the dimension of history, and allow ourselves to keep turning full circle without apparently being conscious of the fact. There is a catchphrase, which once everyone used to mumble, about not bringing education into politics or politics into education. It is meaningless, not just because the two are inextricably linked as a result of the money provided by taxpayers and ratepayers, but also because the State has actively set the educational system clear social obligations.

Moments of despair about the British economy are repeatedly the times when the educational system comes under most scrutiny. Given our current economic health, it was inevitable that the nature and role of education should be the centre of fierce debate. The intervention of a Prime Minister may be new, but a 'great debate' which focuses on the question of whether the educational system is too academic and insufficiently geared to the requirements of industry and commerce has been a frequent phenomenon since the onset of the Industrial Revolution. Contrary to common mythology the State has never been backward in leading such debates.

Strong though the commitment to freedom has been in our universities, the tone and direction of their development has been determined more by the State than by self-generating factors. Even the cherished freedom of staff to teach and research at will stems from their release by the Exchequer from the constraints imposed by lack of cash and dependence on fees. Government has also played a key role in maintaining standards. In the mid-nineteenth century, an awareness of the more sophisticated systems of higher education on the Continent – a realization promoted by Prince Albert – led to enquiries and calls for reform[1].

The result was the shedding of much lower-level work and the development of 'honours' examinations and more professional courses. The State forced the country's higher education institutions away from the social élitism which had awarded places to men of wealth and status but little

131

intelligence, and towards the specialized academic élitism which we traditionally associate with a university today. It was again the government which between the Wars proposed to the universities the desirability of establishing the PhD, in the light of the general belief that Britain was still lagging behind Germany and the United States.

Just as the State has repeatedly seen fit to step in to restructure the edifice or change the direction of the constituent parts, so too, from time to time, it has engineered the growth of the system: by upgrading in the 1950s the low-status university colleges of the 1930s; by creating nine new universities and upgrading the Colleges Advanced Technology in the 1960s: and by establishing a parallel public sector range of institutions in the form of the thirty polytechnics. A concomitant of such expansion has of course been a demand for greater accountability, particularly today as the economy struggles from crisis to crisis.

Any movement towards 'universal'[2] higher education will have to be State-sponsored: it will not come from the institutions themselves. Indeed the perception which academics have of universities is cautious and conservative in the extreme, and probably more opposition to the massive expansion of the 1960s came from the universities themselves than ever was generated in the political system[3]. I would argue, however, that there is no reason to suppose that any government will consciously move towards universal higher education. I would go further and say that in a conventional sense the attempt should not even be made. Though the higher educational system of this country is once again at a point of significant change requiring active government leadership, it is not just a matter of further expansion of traditional degree courses for eighteen-year olds. We must ensure that the result is a system of learning very different from the traditional one. The emphasis has to be swung decisively towards catering for adult learners.

There is essentially no real pressure for government to aim for universal access. In the first place, for both Government and Opposition the politics of education lies in the area of the schools; this is where the controversies are, and this is where it is thought the votes lie. Moreover, the Department of Education and Science is still overwhelmingly a schools-orientated Ministry, rationalized on the basis that attention and resources have to be focused there because the law requires it. It has meant that not much attention has been paid to devising alternative strategies in post-secondary education. The re-organization of the Colleges of Education was a classic example: with apparently little thought given to alternative roles for the resulting Institutions of Higher Education and none, it seems, as to what educational use to make of those colleges that were closed. What we need is a longer range focus.

The implications of the birth rate on the whole of the higher educational system seem at last to have been recognized[4], but so late in the day that all prevailing policy assumptions will have to be thrown out – which is ironical considering that their dominance has prevented any real alternatives being thought through. Adversity, it seems, is a better instructor than prosperity. Merely to hold the proportion of the age group entering higher education in the early eighties to present levels would entail such a crash capital building programme that a Secretary of State is unlikely to get Cabinet approval when resources are so limited. Since these facilities would only just be coming into use as the size of the eighteen to twenty-two age group starts to shrink with increasing momentum (births since 1964 having dropped by a third), ministers will have no justification for proceeding. Nevertheless, as I shall demonstrate, the ideas and approach adopted in the 1960s still form the substance of official thinking.

It is not just that government has an inevitably short-term perspective, it is also that there has been a concern with the *application* of knowledge and the teaching of skills deemed appropriate to a high-technology industrial society. There is a widespread, ill-defined belief, that in some way Britain's inadequate industrial performance relates to a malaise in education. The fact that the Japanese can beat the pants off us in cars and electronics probably arises from socio-philosophical factors of which educational attitudes are only one component. But we are currently pursuing an age-old ambition to attune the British educational system to the needs of productive industry. Time and again this philosophy has come up against the equally powerful notion that education is really about the development of the whole being – frequently the cry of the teaching unions but also widely subscribed to by those ministers and civil servants who have themselves experienced the type of public school and Oxbridge education which embodies the concept.

The two philosophies have always pulled at higher education, and although the DES has never been equipped to undertake much in the way of radical long-term planning procedures[5], it is salutary to remember that planning requires agreement about goals. In the House of Commons there are a handful of MPs who see eye to eye on the principles on which a comprehensive long-term strategy might be based. A consensus on goals, if not on the sequence of steps to reach them, might just be possible. But I am far from sanguine that very much is going to change in the near future.

In Britain debate is becoming a substitute for action. The decisiveness of government will have to improve upon present practice. For one thing there will have to be greater coherence of ministerial direction than we have been accustomed to in recent years. During the first two and a half years of Harold Wilson's third government, there were twelve ministerial changes at the DES, and Gerry Fowler's career as Minister of State established a new 'law of diminishing tenure': three times in the same job – eight months, seven months and six months!

At present, however, 'relevance' is in the saddle and is unlikely to be supplanted in the short term. This is not another brief love affair between a Labour Government and technology, as we had in the sixties. The political imperatives of the day are value for money and better manpower planning, and both political parties are infected.

The Prime Minister asks whether education, irrespective of level, has become divorced from the needs of an industrial society. But the call for utility and expertise has been heard many times in the past 150 years. In 1828 the Utilitarians founded University College, London; in 1966 Tony Crosland launched the polytechnics. To all of them the universities looked increasingly irrelevant to the needs of the day. In 1851 business interests backed Owen's College, which later became the University of Manchester[6]. And the out-datedness of the universities was poignantly captured by Herbert Spencer, who, writing in 1869, accused them of 'mumbling little else but dead formulae'[7].

To read one of the Board of Education Reports of the early years of this century carries with it a strong sense of *deja vu*. 'There is little doubt that the commercial prosperity of the country during recent years', stated the Report for 1911–12, 'has had a good deal to do with this diminution in the number of students who are seeking a university education'[8]. At the time, Oxford and Cambridge were distinctly orientated in favour of disciplines thought appropriate for leadership at home and in the Empire, the tone being set by the neo-Platonists at Balliol. In one sense, of course, it was a curriculum with a vocational objective, but strictly speaking these vocational courses were restricted to the liberal professions of the law, medicine and the church. They did not easily take to the sciences. Even at Cambridge, it was unusual for a scientist to be made a Fellow of a college.

On the other hand, the new 'provincial' universities were seen as a different range of institutions altogether. Board of Education reports indicate that the role of these 'young' universities was pitched firmly in the world of commerce. Indeed, some of them were based on old urban colleges and their backing came from local business communities.

Yet in this continual tug of war between intellectualism and vocationalism, the former has always kept its supremacy. And despite measures like the Technical Education Act of 1889, or the creation of the CATs in the late fifties, technical education has never fared as well in Britain as it has on the Continent. Successive 'new' institutions readily adopted the traditions and values of Oxbridge. Even their physical features have been reproduced, however unnecessarily or inappropriately – whether it be in the design of the early halls of residence, or in the choice of rivers and lakes for the new campuses which were built in the 1960s.

Looking at the positioning of the 'new' universities of that time, one begins to wonder whether the planners had ever become aware of the shift of economic power from countryside to industrial town. Like Matthew Arnold, they seemed to feel that the realities of urban industrial life were too brutish for the refinements of the mind. A cloistered community of scholars was clearly their guiding image. This is not to say that there is anything wrong in according esteem to scholarship and research, only that all of higher education should not be geared in that direction.

The one Oxbridge feature above all others which has set the style of British universities has been the notion of a community of scholars. Even in the Scottish universities where, apart from St. Andrews, the tradition was to accept local students, it has taken a firm hold in the last decade. Throughout the system as a result, there has been a steady erosion of the proportion of students who are home-based. In 1935 the proportion was 54·9 per cent (excluding Oxford and Cambridge). In 1950 it was 43·8 per cent, in 1960 it was down to 25.9 per cent, in 1970 it was 17·5 per cent, in 1974 it was 17.1 per cent, and in 1976 it was 16.0 per cent[9]. Such a pattern is particularly expensive because it requires a large amount of purpose-built accommodation and the provision of a whole range of facilities such as student unions, which currently cost over £16 million a year in fees. Moreover, there is a great deal of public cynicism about the value of university expenditure in general. The attitude that more must mean worse has been well entrenched on the Right Wing of the Conservative Party. But the far Left too has ended its romance with higher education. They see precious resources, which could be benefiting the schools, and the unemployed sixteen- to nineteen-year olds in particular, going to, as they see it, the narrow social élite in the universities. Each party contains awkward anti-higher education groups, while there is little in the way of a strong pro-lobby.

For some time there has been no official mention of the 22 per cent target for the proportion of the eighteen-year age group entering higher education which was the cornerstone of the 1972 White Paper[10] and which at the time was assailed by many as being inadequate. For the last seven years interest in higher education has stayed steady[11]. In 1977–8 the proportion of the age-group entering higher education was about $13\frac{1}{2}$ per cent, and the present target is merely to step that up to $14\frac{1}{2}$ per cent by

135

1981–2. However, the 22 per cent target *could* become a reality in the mid-1990s, if somewhat by default.

Merely to provide places for about the current proportion of qualified school leavers throughout the period of the 'bulge' (the eighteen-year old age group does not decline until 1982–3) could entail a £200 million capital building programme. Recurrent costs, including student grants would total over £100 million extra a year. Most of this expansion need not, of course, take place in the university sector, and if two-year courses in the non-university sector could be made more popular, costs would be less. But, essentially, the sheer cost per place of the traditional British pattern of higher education will make it impossible for any government to contemplate expansion to anything like twice the present size.

In the unlikely event of the government undertaking expansion to meet the 'bulge' and an economic revival making contraction unnecessary, then *de facto* we would take a major jump towards a 'universal' system. Even if this were desirable, there must be a doubt about the success of such a course. The relative demand for particular types of education will vary considerably and will certainly be unpredictable. On present form, however, sluggish interest on the part of sixth formers will mean that overall there will be no guarantee of capacity being filled for we would need to achieve a fifty per cent increase on the present proportion entering higher education. The less prestigious institutions would almost certainly have to lower the standard of entry. This is a prospect that is deeply worrying to Conservatives. And though Conservative eyes have been slow to open to the alternatives, it is now increasingly felt that it would be better to make changes in the composition of the student body and in the goals higher education has hitherto sought to meet. It seems however, that the process of educational planning is not good at the re-definition of objectives.

The Robbins Report on Higher Education in 1963 marked the ultimate expression of the commitment to liberal concepts of higher education[12]. Alternatively, it can be viewed as the last victory of the traditionalists before the resurgence of vocationalism, which began within five years of Robbins reporting and which reached its apogee in Lord Crowther-Hunt and the Prime Minister's Ruskin speech[13]. Ironically, it opened the way to the expansion of British higher education from an 'élite' to a 'mass' system. The logic of its philosophy that 'courses of higher education should be available for all those who are qualified by ability and attainment to pursue them and who wish to do so', was an open-ended commitment to 'universal' access.

The number of those qualified and willing to enter higher education grew more rapidly up to the early 1970s than the Robbins Committee expected. But thereafter, the rate of growth fell, and the recent pick-up might only be a reflection of the very poor job prospects facing school-leavers. So, even if there had not been a collapse in teacher education provision, achieving a 'universal' system has never seemed very likely.

The Robbins Report embodied a paradoxical mixture of radicalism and traditionalism for it never challenged the assumption that the content would be that of the earlier élitist pattern. It was not a report which questioned at all the nature of higher education, and, given the composition of the Committee, it naturally did not question the appropriateness for the future of the existing style. Utilitarian considerations were tersely dismissed; character development was clearly regarded as part of the process of higher education; and education was viewed not as a means to some other end but as an end in itself.

The attitude of Conservatives to this was somewhat ambivalent. The Robbins view of the nature of higher education was essentially in line with Conservative thinking at the time. The Conservative Party has always regarded the expansion of educational opportunities with favour; education has been seen in terms of providing a path to personal liberty – as against the Left-wing's view of education as a great equalizer; and there has existed a general belief that without a well-developed educational system, freedom and self-government would perish. Yet at the same time, there were many Conservatives who questioned the likely impact of such a fast rate of expansion on academic standards. Though it was the Macmillan Government which in the late fifties planned the new Universities of Sussex, York, Warwick, Lancaster, Essex, Kent and East Anglia, many Conservative backbenchers instinctively felt that more meant worse[14]. This is still an element to be contended with. The Robbins Report might have argued for the radical notion that higher education thresholds could be crossed by numbers of pupils hitherto undreamed of, but it has not convinced the bulk of the Conservative Party of the merits of 'universal' access.

The trouble with both Parties is that there is much in their rhetoric which is attractive but neither talks often in practical terms. There is no point, on the one hand, in talking in terms of abstract principles of redistributive justice. Equally, there is not much to be gained by the Right preaching the worth of market forces and the benefits of vouchers – they are not within the realms of current political possibility. There is one basic utilitarian consideration that matters deeply to Conservatives, however, and one which is, in some form or other, often heard. And that is that the pursuit of wider opportunities must be achieved without impairing the quality of the provision available for those who can really benefit from it; the said justification being that these people will then make a better contribution to the needs of their fellow men. In educational policy as in the industrial arena, the Conservative view tends instinctively to be that one should back winners. It is felt deeply that able people should be educated to the limits of their ability in order to enable them to make the best of that ability. The Conservative Party is instinctively élitist but these days in a strongly meritocratic sense. Whereas on the Left, the educational system has always been at the centre of social policy development, an instrument of greater equality, offering a cure for a whole range of social problems.

Ever since Robbins, British higher educational planning has been on the basis of the potential numbers of school-leavers with given 'A' level attainment. Places, it has been argued, should then be made available to all who achieved this level, regardless of what they want to do. Ironically, such a market responsive policy today receives little favour from the Conservative Right Wing, whom one would normally expect to endorse such an approach. Clearly the policy has resulted in a proliferation of arts and social science courses and a collapse in the areas of science and technology[15]. Apart from the public expenditure implications, it is this which has given rise to most criticisms of the Robbins formula.

In addition, it is argued that logically it will produce a system akin to the escalator pattern of education which we see in the United States, in which the goal of more and more young people is to stay on and on at school, and then for more and more to move into the universities, and ultimately for higher proportions to undertake Master's and Doctor's courses. Ironically, once universal entry is attained, its relative worth is diminished and so the target moves on a stage, penalising those who fail to make it even more[16]. In no fundamental way, therefore, does it satisfy the Left's goal of diminishing social inequality. In the process, the university changes its character, as it faces up to the needs of a more and more heterogeneous student population. The Conservative Party has therefore stuck firmly to the binary concept – only that now, as a result of the reorganization of the Colleges of Education, a *tripartite* system of higher education has been created, and as I shall argue shortly, in no real sense is there any longer a firm binary line with respect to the courses being offered.

Considering the Conservative Party's closeness to the industrial world, the non-university sector has never been viewed very enthusiastically by many in the Party, in part at least because until recently the Parliamentary Party has almost literally embodied Oxbridge, so that there has been a large element of false nostalgia as to what higher education should be about. In official pronouncements the universities are always emphasized as the 'crown' of our educational system, but Conservative spokesmen, especially when in office, have always promoted the expansion of the applied, polytechnic sector[17].

The balance that has therefore been struck by the Party is not, I think, an unreal one. The problems of manpower forecasting are gigantic, and trying to match forecasts to higher education suffers, as we have seen, from too long a lead time. Though the validity of the 1960s argument that education investment was good for economic growth has been challenged, some link surely does exist. Modern society does make enormous demands upon qualified manpower; demands which, in the quest for improved productivity, are ever growing. Businessmen are calling for recruits with better and better standards in the '3 Rs', just as they were in the years leading up to the 1870 Education Act. And more and more jobs require higher technical skills. So, like it or not, the State is bound to indulge in some sort of broad manpower planning. It is bound to say that for the good of all we need, for example, more doctors, and therefore we shall concentrate resources in order to produce them. The current fashion, of course, is to say that we need more engineers, and we have seen the policy flowing from that; notably the decision of the Government, and its instant implementation by the University Grants Committee (UGC), to found new four-year élite engineering courses.

The balance that the Conservative Party has struck is based on the assumption that a pluralist society requires a plural education system. There is no one 'best answer' when so much is unforeseen or unforeseeable. There is no intrinsic merit in seeking a pattern of higher education which aims to have everybody going along the same route, namely, admission to a university. Moreover, it is crazy to suppose ensuring equality of provision is in itself fair and just. Either the opportunities offered enable those with the inclination and ability to become more unequal, or else it becomes designed as a handicap race for the ablest. In fact, the logic inherent in a universal higher educational system often seems to pass unnoticed; namely, that the inclusion of everyone, even if attainable, cannot prevent selectivity. For some will advance further and faster than others; some will learn more than others; some will become more skilful than others; and some will develop better judgement than others. It cannot, therefore, distribute life-chances more equitably.

The mere extension of a system is not an answer. Starting at the secondary level, there must come a point when it is neither educationally valuable nor socially beneficial to encourage people to stay in school. The Conservative Party feels that the point has been reached; indeed that there should be sufficient flexibility that the last year of secondary education need not be taken in school at all. The same is true at eighteen. As opportunities to enter university become universal, so the *necessity* of entering becomes universalized. It ceases to be a matter of open choice; for the more who go, the more one is penalizing those who do not. Conservatives would argue that the traditional three-year academic degree course is not the best route for all school leavers to follow. Nor, for that matter, does it seem to be one which appeals to a large number of eighteen-year olds even though the pressures in society that influence parents, teachers and employers to believe that entry to a university is a must if at all possible, are still strong, and the misfiring of the student grant system makes it the best paid route to take. To be able to break the expectation of immediate entry to higher education from school would not only have a pronounced effect on student motivation, but would significantly reduce the pressure on places during the period of the 'bulge'.

With individualism embedded so deeply in its ideology, the Conservative Party stands committed to a range of opportunities which individuals can opt for according to their inclinations and aptitude – 'diversity of provision to match the diversity of human need' – was the way I once summed it up in a keynote speech[18]. Within this the Conservative aim, therefore, is to extend existing institutional diversity and make it more dynamic by creating incentives for greater flexibility, and encouraging institutional initiative.

The open access university is a goal of the Left, but an anathema to Conservatives[19]. We question the capacity of a university to go on making the distinctive contribution it is, if its student body becomes more and more heterogeneous. Though more may not mean worse, it certainly means different. The type and level of its courses must change to meet the vastly different needs and tastes of a widening range of enrolments. Already this pressure is being felt, and in the United States there is an increasing criticism of the results of such an open access policy.

On the one hand, therefore, the Conservative Party defends the concept of the university as a place for developing certain qualities of mind, while at the same time wanting institutions in which instruction is less centred around the traditionally organized disciplines of knowledge.

For want of a better way of putting it, university education is nothing if it is not of the highest *intellectual* quality. Any system of higher education must be able to offer those of highest ability the means to study in depth a specialized academic subject. It is crucial for maintaining the intellectual health of the country through scholarship and research. The essence of a university is that it need not be instantly responsive to politically defined ends; even though they may become more so in their search for government funds, their goals can still be self-generated. Membership of the university thereby offers freedom for untrammelled thought and discussion, the ability to sit back and think from first principles or to develop original ideas and challenge conventional wisdom. They are also institutions which enable society to maintain certain values and standards. Our universities are widely admired throughout the world, and wastage rates are extraordinarily low. All of this ought to be preserved.

Equally obvious, not everyone can or should sit back and contemplate, or seek after eternal truths. Society, therefore, needs institutions which, to use Dr Patrick Nutgen's words, can provide an education 'informed by action rather than inert knowledge'[20]. It will not do to teach only principles; skills and techniques are also needed.

These different roles co-exist in any given institution. There is now an enormous overlap between the work of the universities and the polytechnics. The university system has itself become far too heterogeneous – ranging from St. David's Lampeter to Loughborough – to be amenable to simple definition or comfortable stereotype. In fact, perceiving the way the political winds have been blowing in favour of utilitarianism, Vice-Chancellors have lost no opportunity to emphasise the university's capacity to respond to modern demands. Only a few years ago, the Vice-Chancellor of Cambridge, at a time when the universities felt particularly on the defensive and confronted by unsympathetic ministers, wrote a long essay on the practical contribution made to society by the country's universities[21]. And impressive it is. Since the war, they have, of course, added a whole galaxy of subjects that an earlier age would not have dreamed respectable for a university to teach. Accountancy, for example, has become one of the fastest growth areas; and there is forestry, horticulture, architecture, dramatic art, transport and nursing, and a host of others. Indeed, although it is conventional to argue that the polytechnics have become progressively more like universities, it may be as valid these days to argue the reverse, namely that to maintain a hold on government funds, universities have become more like polytechnics. Most of the applied subjects on which, by their terms of reference, polytechnics are meant to concentrate, are today to be found in the universities, especially so in those which formerly were the Colleges of Advanced Technology.

Though we cannot make facile categorizations, labels which embrace organizations of varied and multiple kinds may still have value in indicating that, though institutions might resemble each other in certain of their parts, they are nevertheless broadly geared to different roles, within which each institution sets itself special tasks to perform. The polytechnics must continue to have that much more of a vocational and local role than the universities. And whereas the universities will *primarily* continue to offer the three-year honours degree, the polytechnics and the new institutions of higher education face a crucial challenge in the provision of short and part-time courses.

Ministers have failed to address themselves to this fundamental question of definition: what sort of courses, what type of student, and what overall size shall be required of each sector. We are apparently in a policy vacuum. The central premises of the Robbins Report that higher education is good in itself and that it is a right for all people, seem to have become impossible to maintain. But they are not discredited, and in the absence of alternatives, are still paid lip-service. There has been no serious effort to re-examine the purposes of higher education in the light of changing times. We have been faced with a kind of policy *ad hocery*, which emerges from political compromises and economic pressures[22].

In its day the Robbins Report had the political sex appeal that was crucial to mobilize government will to enable higher education to catch up with the school population. It also benefited from the political environment at that time: with a Conservative Government near a general election wanting to satisfy the increasing awareness by parents of the economic and social value of higher education qualifications, and keen to head off the Labour Party's charge that Britain was falling behind in the international league table of higher education.

At the present time there are quite different political imperatives. With such high unemployment rates amongst young people, the Trade Union Congress (TUC) and internal Party pressures have obliged the Labour Government to channel resources to the Manpower Services Commission, even though its initiatives have been almost exclusively focused on short-term measures, without much thought given to education's contribution in the longer term.

Very seldom, it seems, do we ever ask what it is overall we are really seeking to do. Government funding has not constituted any real setting of policy. Does anyone ask: 'Is what we are trying to do in this particular area, squaring with our overall vision for the future?'. Take for example, the proposals for the sixteen to nineteen age group, scattered as they are between the DES, the Manpower Services Commission, the Training Services Agency (TSA), and the local authorities. What is the distinctiveness of this group, compared say with the twenty to twenty-four age group, which actually forms a higher proportion of the unemployed total? Or take the decision on university fees for overseas students, which rebounded through the whole of higher education and resulted in, at the end of the day, not only untold and unforeseen damage to self-supporting, part-time and mature students, but in something like £3½ million being handed out to pay the fees of even the wealthiest British families.

In the midst of an economic recession and the heavy retrenchment which education above all services has seen, morale is poor and there is little sense of vision. Yet an overall strategy for the development of all post-secondary provision that looks at least twenty years ahead is as crucial during a time of retrenchment as it is in planning expansion. Already however, our room for manoeuvre has been limited by decisions reached long before the document *Higher Education into the 1990s* was produced. Even this paper is primarily concerned with patching up the system and minimising the effects of the collapsing birth rate. We seem stuck with the terms of reference drawn up by Robbins. Its discussion of alternative approaches, such as drawing in greater numbers of women and mature students, sees them as 'expedients'. One is left with the feeling that its authors have searched for ways of trying at all costs to keep intact the Robbins philosophy, albeit in a watered-down form. It is characterized by old cautions, not new horizons.

It is a harsh fact of life that Oppositions primarily strike policy positions in response to Government statements, but with regard to the future, the basis of the Conservative policy work has been to attempt to establish principles other than numbers on which to develop higher education; the key one being that education is not just something which happens to youngsters.

Every new idea is, of course, an incitement to spend. And in the present economic climate this makes the problem of persuasion difficult for educationists in the Conservative Party. But the starting point has to be what is it we, as individuals and as a nation, need, and what are the steps we can afford? The central questions that have to be addressed are: what is it that people need that they are not able now to get through established patterns of education? What sort of people are they? What are the kinds of opportunities which they might respond to? How far can these new opportunities be presented to people by using existing rather than additional facilities? Merely trying to give more of the same, only with fewer resources – the depressing scene which has confronted the universities for the last five years – will not be satisfactory.

If we cast our gaze forward, we can see one thing for certain: the pace of change in society will go on accelerating. Our economic, social and moral environment is being transformed by scientific progress. Since the War, the speed of scientific and technological advance, and the sheer growth of knolwedge, has been phenomenal. Despite all that has been written about it,

Part Four: The Political Implications

I do not believe that people yet appreciate what is happening. The seemingly impossible is being realized in a shorter and shorter space of years. So dramatic have been some of the developments, such as space exploration, that it is easy to become blasé, to accept as commonplace things that were unthinkable to pre-war generations.

So the long-term objective we have to aim for is surely clear enough. Since the challenge each of us faces is constantly going to be transformed, education must have a key role in offering the opportunities to help us adjust. In order to meet the demands of a large number of different types of people, we will have to turn our post-secondary educational system into a new mould, to give it a recurrent dimension. In other words, to give all age groups the opportunities to re-enter the formal educational and training system at times and places and in ways of their own choosing. This entails a break with existing policies, which are geared to providing more of the same 'end-on' system.

What recurrent or continuing education means, depends in large measure on who is using the terminology, where they come from and the sort of people for whom they have to frame their agendas. For one thing I have never particularly liked the use of the term 'continuing' education because of the impression it conveys of students staying on year after year. And it is the selling of the idea which is the crucial first step. A certain political adroitness is necessary in pitching the arguments. To the Left it may have appeal as a vehicle for equalising life-chances and offsetting early disadvantage. In many writings it has a satisfying if imprecise ring to it.

The Conservative Party tends to show impatience at vague theorizing. Yet for a Party which places such weight on individualism, the concept of recurrent education ought to have great appeal. As individuals we need change; we need variety; we need to refresh our minds; to keep our skills in trim. Increasingly what we learn in our youth will be quickly outdated, and people will therefore need an educational system which prepares them for change. It also offers a great new second chance to those who missed out during the long years of schooling. And it will give each one of us the chance to simply take an educational break: an interplay of education and other work which might help us to keep up with the needs of our jobs, but also to cope better with pressures, perhaps. It presents opportunities for those who want to get on by offering them the means to improve qualifications – and the Tory belief in freedom means freedom to achieve as well as freedom from restraint. Women, for example, are no longer so willing to devote a life-time to the home and the family. In educational terms, recurrent education makes it unnecessary to try to cram everything into school and university: it halts the escalator. Politically, for a Party which is instinctively sceptical of planning the future, a recurrent educational system plans for uncertainty. It does not prescribe, and has the flexibility not to be tied to the fashions of the day, which are so easily the disasters of tomorrow. And in social terms it has the potential to transform the whole texture of British life, breaking down class rigidities, and releasing a flood of human ability. But the point that has to be grasped is that resources will only be made available if it can tap the new interest in vocational education. In this context it is worth noting that sixty per cent of adult learners in America undertake courses for occupational reasons. If this is accepted as a working hypothesis, it does of course raise the highly pertinent question of how to ensure that the design of courses reflects the needs of the customer rather than the subject specialist![23]

How then to move the system over to this new approach? It will be a pretty herculean task. And no 'big bang' theory of reform will get very far. The reason is simple: traditional attitudes are deeply entrenched, and there is no money for a global approach. The way forward can only be by developing a series of complementary activities on a number of fronts. 'Big bang' solutions may be strong in intellectual or emotional appeal, but are desperately weak in application and applicability. Only incremental changes, not sweeping transformations, have a chance of gaining Tory support. Though each initiative should be seen as part and parcel of the longer-term objective (a full recurrent system of post-secondary education) they would be valuable in themselves. They must be seen, as well as planned, as part of the whole, however. For the important thing is to get the concept of adult learning legitimized, broadly accepted and brought within the domain of public policy formulation.

Then there is the central question of resources. At a time when Vice-Chancellors feel that consolidation, rather than expansion with proportionately fewer resources, would be no bad thing, university numbers should be held at about the 300,000 to 350,000 mark (the only exception is for women where further expansion is necessary). Moreover, part-time work in the universities is so small (less than ten per cent overall) that some expansion without heavy additional outlay ought to be possible. Higher education in the public sector has not been as cost-effective or as good as it should have been, but whether the Oakes Committee's proposals will do enough to rationalize the system is doubtful[24].

To prevent any significant loss of opportunity if the university system is stabilized, there must be an immediate drive to make alternative roads more attractive. In the absence of clear policy guidelines, there has been

145

disastrous 'academic drift' in much of the non-university sector – although not in the polytechnics, eighty per cent of whose work is still strictly vocational – but in the newly created Institutions of Higher Education and in some Further Education Colleges. Frankly, we need more of the type of three-year degree courses they are now establishing as much as we need a hole in the head! What we have to make more attractive are the technician level courses – the HND and TEC's and BEC's new Higher Diplomas, and the Dip.HE – which are central to this country's prospects. The Institutions of Higher Education should, even at this late stage, be required to become primarily two-year institutions which offer vocational courses in, say, computing or the paramedical services, or form a jumping-off point for people to move on to a degree course elsewhere.

Below the technician level, there is a substantial group receiving a combination of further education and training designed to fit them for skilled occupations in industry or corresponding levels of skill in commerce. There is considerable scope for reform and improvement in this area, particularly in regard to age of entry, duration, and recognition of adult retraining, and progress is held up by the collective bargaining machinery of industry. This too, is a priority area for government intervention.

In pursuing incentives for non-degree level courses, the student grant system must be overhauled. In fact every aspect of it is riddled with anomalies. Parents are expected to make a semi-voluntary payment for the higher education of their 'adult' children, but the majority of parents cannot or will not pay all their supposed contribution; so unless the government is deliberately trying to hold down the numbers entering higher education by a method which has the effect of discriminating against the poorer paid middle-class and better-off manual workers, a change of policy is called for. The Departments of Education, of Social Security and of Employment and the Manpower Services Commission have acted in isolation from each other. Like Topsy, the system just growed. So tangled are the financial arrangements that they form a major disincentive at every level. Young people, though keen to take a course, find they get more money from the State by doing nothing than if they receive a minor discretionary award, since financial restraint has made many local authorities less generous in the use of their discretion and their willingness to interpret the rules favourably, especially for non-traditional short courses lasting for a month or two.

Fees for part-time courses have shot up, and no incentives are forth-coming to encourage young people to think of part-time courses as valid alternatives. As Professor Dahrendorf put it 'the grant system in Britain is rigged in favour of the bored youngster; nobody who wakes up a little late in life and discovers that he or she is actually interested has a chance'[25]. On the one hand, mature postgraduates are reluctant to take up a full-time course because the grant they are offered is insufficient to meet their commitments: a family man cannot live with the life-style of an eighteen-year old. On the other, they are unlikely to find money for part-time courses. In 1974–5 only 169 of Birkbeck College's 961 part-time postgraduates had an award; 45 from private employers, and only two of the rest were not seconded teachers.

Why should part-timers not be entitled to financial support? It would be worth it, for part-time costs are below half full-time[26]. Moreover, whether they are studying at the technician or degree level, or taking a part-time short professional course, these students are paying tax and National Insurance, and because they live at home, they make no demands on public funds for maintenance. And since adults have an independent life outside of the university or college, to which they go for a specific purpose not for the social life, costly student union facilities are less necessary.

Ministers have displayed a totally negative attitude to part-time education over a long period. It is not just cheaper, it is more flexible and offers the individual, especially married women, greater choice. And given the Tory Party's philosophy, there is a strong case for a Conservative Government giving positive encouragement to the self-supporting student. In part-time courses a student learns by facing the responsibilities of an actual job. Admittedly, he may be under enormous pressure, but that in itself ensures that the student makes the best use of his time. Above all the motivation of someone already in a job and seeking to advance his or her career is likely to be better than that of a traditional straight-from-school entrant. And it is vital that Britain's long tradition of advancing oneself through learning on the job is maintained and strengthened.

The danger of thinking of 'universal' higher education in conventional terms is that part-time education will continue to be thought of as a make-shift, a stop-gap whilst we await the millenium of universal full-time education. It must not be so. On the contrary, it should be central to our entire educational strategy. There is a strong likelihood, however, that politicians will be unable to resist concentrating on full-time provision simply because it acts as a buffer against massive youth unemployment.

Nothing will be achieved unless the incentive/disincentive equation is altered. Without total reform of all grants and fees we will stay caught in a vicious circle of low demand and a poor supply. Through the TOPS programme and the Industrial Training Boards, the MSC has become the major financier of openings for adult learners, but from the perspective of the unemployment position; its schemes are not permanent, and they are not conceived in the context of a recurrent educational system. All the DES is able to do is to urge people to take courses for three days a week so that they can retain social security payments[27]. If we could devize a policy which gave financial support for part-time work when at least one year had been spent in a job, it would have a double benefit by dramatically easing the pressure on higher education places during the 'bulge' years. At the very least, by reducing from twenty-five to twenty-one the age at which students are regarded for grant purposes as independent of their parents, eighteen-year olds might be induced to gain wider experience before entry into higher education.

Already costing £350 million a year, the student grant system could become the greatest hindrance to the extension of higher education. Whether any party will be able to summon up the courage to examine the potential of loans, is very doubtful. But it should not be excluded merely on the basis of longstanding opposition from groups like the National Union of Students. The self-supporting mature student might welcome it if the option is high fees and a bank overdraft. Without for the moment thinking of the traditional degree student, expansion of short, professional course and part-time or correspondence learning might require student loans, the interest of which would be tax deductible as is the case with housing loans of up to £25,000. If the commercial banks could be drawn on for such a scheme, it would result in an enormous injection of cash into higher education. And anything which gives greater latitude and flexibility of choice to the individual should be tried. On present trends what will happen is that as fees go up there will be tremendous pressure to match them automatically with grants (by definition a wasteful policy); and since the value is unlikely to be maintained in real terms, by default – because of the non-payment of parental contribution – the cost of running higher education will fall increasingly on parents.

Equally, it will be necessary to develop incentives for the institutions. The Burnham salary scales have created a powerful incentive for teaching full-time students, and more weighting will have to be given to part-time work. Although mature students bring a valuable range of experience to a university, UGC funding arrangements do not recognize these short, up-dating courses. And if the student cannot find the fees, industry is these days not in much of a position to do so either. It is the same story with sandwich courses. The extra costs involved are not met by the UGC, and although the Department of Employment has improved matters, there is still no scheme for assisting the placement of students for work experience. Concessions on tax or national insurance contributions might be the only way to give the necessary boost to block-release, sponsorship or placement programmes, but will any Education Secretary be able to persuade the Treasury?

There are two other essential developments which will not be readily accepted. Admission policies will need to be loosened to allow in mature students who have demonstrated their ability by actual performance but may not have the traditional 'O' and 'A' level requirements. And transferability between different courses, levels and institutions, with credit given for courses already completed, will have to be made more of a reality than it has become so far, thanks to the initiatives of the Open University. Part-timers will want to accelerate their progress towards their final qualification; and various means such as transfers into full-time courses or summer school bridging courses will have to be thought about.

Faced with their family and work commitments, adult students cannot fit into a traditional pattern of residential higher education. We will have to cater for the commuting student – providing more modest, more localized opportunities, and searching for new techniques which extend opportunities without demanding excessive new resources. The ultimate logic is to make learning a much more individualistic activity. The Open University has demonstrated what can be done. Directed private study, involving correspondence learning combined with face-to-face tuition, presents many possibilities, especially in the light of the new teaching technology such as CEEFAX. Taking instruction to the actual place of work, possibly using the equipment on the spot, is another possibility.

It is vital to snap out of the 'progress equals building' mentality. Given present public expenditure restraints, it can do nothing other than distract thought from developing alternative 'soft' strategies. What are the mechanics of persuading people that status lies not in the newness of buildings, but in the type and quality of the teaching? Models exist in the United States which would be worth trying on a pilot basis; the notion for example of a 'university without walls', which involves teaching staff presenting courses out in the community – in school halls or rented facilities of any kind wherever there is a demand[28]. Universities and polytechnics might become resource centres for a wide range of further and adult education establishments. Their staff, as in the Open University tutoring system, being paid to supplement the teaching in a neighbouring establishment.

In this way, higher education could reach out to a great many more people, create a comprehensive market of provision that brings together existing resources, public and private, presenting courses at convenient times and places so that the individual is given the maximum scope to choose what best fits his or her circumstances. The public of course would have to have information and advice on all the possibilities open to them in

149

some readily accessible form. Responsibility for devising this should fall on the new Council for Adult and Continuing Education. In truth, however, this body should be a *development* council, not merely an advisory one. Look at the enormous individual, and institutional, creativity and energy that was released by the Adult Literacy Resources Agency, despite the smallness of its budget! We do not want more creeping regulation and control by a central Department, but I do believe that the only way that we shall establish a framework of positive inducements for the developments I have outlined is if there is a catalyst agency which by pump-priming funds could stimulate fresh thinking, and could back good ideas by matched funding. Without such a new enabling mechanism we are likely merely to drift on. Such times as these, times of difficulty and doubt, can also be times of opportunity, provided there is leadership which is clear-sighted and which has courage and tenacity. But there are many faint hearts.

There is a great tendency in our nation, every time a project of an imaginative kind comes up, not to take it in hand, but to procrastinate in the face of those who, as soon as it shows signs of being difficult or presenting problems as well as advantages, or is simply expensive, immediately urge a fresh look and back away. It is time we turned a deaf ear to the faint hearts and the sentimentalists who criticize every enterprise on the ground that it is too disturbing. The ideas I have put forward here present many difficulties; they offer even more new possibilities. But they call for decisions to be taken now, and that requires leadership. Yet all the signs are that we will struggle through the next six years or so on broadly the same lines as now in order to see what 'turns up' in the mid-eighties. It is an inertia that has become a debilitating disease in too many areas of government, and one which might well prevent us from grasping the full majesty of the opportunities that face us.

Notes

[1] *Parliamentary Papers*, XXII, i, 1852, and XLIV, i, 1852–3, for the Report of the Commissioners appointed to enquire into the *State ... of the University and Colleges of Oxford*, and the *Report on the State ... of the University and Colleges of Cambridge*.

[2] For the purpose of this Paper I assume that British higher education has moved from an 'élite' to a 'mass' system, both because of the percentage of the age group which enters it and because it has become characterized by élitist universities expanding to perform a great variety of new functions, a growing range of different institutions, and diverse standards. 'Universal' higher education is achieved when between fifty and eighty per cent of the age group proceed from school into some form of higher education.

[3] A.H. Halsey and M. Trow, *The British Academic*, Faber and Faber, 1971, p. 464.

[4] See Department of Education and Science, *Higher Education into the 1990s: A Discussion Document*, February 1978.

[5] For criticisms of DES Planning, see 'Educational Development Strategy in England and Wales', OECD, 1975, and the *Tenth Report from the Expenditure Committee*, 'Policy Making in the Department of Education & Science', 29 July 1976.

[6] See H. Bellot, *University College, London, 1826–1926*, Athlone Press, 1929; and H.B. Charlton, *Portrait of a University*, Manchester University Press, 1951.

[7] Herbert Spencer, *Education, Intellectual, Moral and Physical*, Thinkers Library ed., 1949, p. 23.

[8] Board of Education, *Reports from Universities receiving Grants, 1912–13*, 1; xi.

[9] Written Answer, 6th February 1976, *Hansard*, Col. 757.

[10] *Education: A Framework for Expansion*, Cmnd. 5174., Dec. 1972.

[11] See *THES*, 27 January 1978, p. 1 for this year's sharp fall in the percentage increase of University applications compared with the previous two years.

[12] *Committee on Higher Education* (Robbins Report), 1963, Cmnd. 2154; see Editorial Comment, *TES*, 23 October 1970 for the expansionist mood of that period.

[13] Lord Crowther-Hunt was Minister of State in the Department of Education and Science from October 1974 to January 1976. The speech at Ruskin College which launched the 'Great Education Debate' was on 18 October, 1976.

[14] See C.B. Cox and A.E. Dyson (eds.), *Fight for Education: a Black Paper*, Critical Quarterly Society, 1969.

[15] From 1965–1970 there was a 16 per cent increase in those taking engineering degrees in universities and a 65 per cent increase in the non-university sector; over the same period there was a 35 per cent increase in those studying Social Sciences and 49 per cent in Arts subjects in the universities and 173 per cent for Social Sciences and 146 per cent for Arts in the public sector.

[16] See Martin Trow, *Problems in the Transition from Elite to Mass Higher Education* (reprint), Carnegie Commission on Higher Education, 1973, p. 8.

[17] *The Right Approach*, Conservative Central Office, October 1976, p. 64; and Norman St. John-Stevas, *Hansard* 13 January 1978, cols. 2054–2064. Mrs. Thatcher's 1972 White Paper envisaged the fastest growth of student numbers being in the Polytechnics, so that by 1981 there would be 375,000 students in each sector.

[18] K. Hampson, MP; speech to the Conservative Women's Annual Conference, 26 May 1976.

[19] This has led the Party to oppose the Labour policy proposals for 'comprehensive' universities accountable to new regional governments.

[20] Dr. P. Nutgens, Director of Leeds Polytechnic, 'Learning to Some Purpose', the Burton Design Award Lecture 1977, p. 20.

[21] Professor J.W. Linnett, '"Useful" Research in Cambridge University', October 1975.

[22] See Tyrell Burgess, *Times Educational Supplement*, 23 October 1970, p. 7.

[23] For an examination of this problem see K. Hampson, 'Bridging the Great Divide: RELAY Centres', in *Advice* (New Opportunity Press), Spring 1978.

[24] See K. Hampson, 'Financing Public Sector Education', in *Public Finance and Accountancy*, October 1977, pp. 341–343.

[25] Ralf Dahrendorf 'FTEs or Higher Madness', in *Times Higher Educational Supplement*, 20 January 1978, p. 7.

[26] Part-time courses in the public sector cost between a third and a half of a full-time equivalent qualification, depending upon the allowance made for wastage rates.

[27] Amendment No. 1 to DES Administrative Memorandum 4/77, *Further Education for Unemployed Young People*. This broadened the long-standing definition of 'three days a week' to mean '21 day-time hours of instruction'. Since this could result in school leavers opting out of the sixth form to take their qualifications in a FE College so that they could collect social security, severe restrictions have been placed on the interpretation of the memorandum, in that a person will be 'expected to take up work if offered even if this should happen just before examinations'!

[28] The Vermont Community College system, for instance, has no 'campus' buildings at all.

9. A Labour View

Gerald Fowler

At the beginning of the 1950s some $3\frac{1}{2}$ per cent of the eighteen-year old age group in Britain entered higher education. By the time of the Robbins Report, in 1963, the proportion had approximately doubled to about 7 per cent. Ten years later it had doubled again, and it has remained consistently at 13 to 14 per cent throughout the mid-1970s[1]. In this respect, Britain has followed what has been a common pattern in Western Europe. In some Western European countries, e.g. Denmark, similar proportions of the age group now attend higher education. In others, the proportion is somewhat higher. In Sweden it is already well over 20 per cent.

In Martin Trow's terminology, Britain is poised to make the transition from élite to mass higher education, if we assume that that transition begins when the proportion of young people entering higher education passes the mid-teens[2]. That would certainly not be the only criterion for deciding that what had been an élite system was changing into a mass system. We should need to look too, for example, at the institutional structure within higher education. Does the bulk of higher education still take place within traditional universities, which have remained relatively small by international standards? In Britain, the answer to that question would be 'Yes', despite the development of the polytechnics and other new institutions of higher education[3]. We should need to look too at the academic structure of courses of higher education. In élite systems, one would expect to find a defined standard of educational achievement upon point of entry, and commonly courses of narrow, but deep and integrated academic content, often leading to professional qualification, and nearly always to a terminal examination designed to measure the attainment by the student of a high and consistent standard. Despite the introduction of some modular degree courses, and other rare innovations, such as a degree by independent study, that is still precisely what we find, not only in the British universities, but also in the public or non-university sector[4].

In an élite system we should expect that power within institutions would reside primarily with senior academic staff, professors, or their equivalents. There would be some professional administrators, but they would be perceived as the servants of the academic community, rather than as those who create the administrative framework to which the educator at the chalkface must conform. New administrative and financial management techniques may have been introduced, but they are not yet perceived as being integral to the control of higher education, as they are likely to be in a much larger system, composed of much larger institutions. This is again precisely what we find in the United Kingdom. In the 1960s there was some broadening of the power structure within institutions of higher education, so that representatives of junior academic staff could take a fuller part in decision-making. As a result of the student troubles of the 1968–70 period, which were much less severe in Britain than in many other Western countries, some token student representation was introduced into the government structure of both universities and non-university colleges, and there is now regular consultation with student representative bodies at both national and institutional levels. In essence however the power structure within higher education has changed little. Further, while there are now more professional administrators than there were at the time of Robbins in the higher education system, and while attempts have been made to introduce more efficient management techniques both in the control of the national system and in the running of individual institutions, the role of the administrator is still perceived as subordinate to that of the academic and educator[5].

That is to say, the UK system of higher education still has most of the marks of an élite system, although there are some signs of the approaching transition to mass higher education. It is a very long way from becoming a 'universal' system, on the pattern already visible in the United States. We may perhaps assume that when 50 per cent of an age cohort enter higher education, whether immediately after the completion of secondary schooling, or after the lapse of some time spent in gaining work experience, which may be as long as ten or fifteen years, then the transition to a universal system is inexorable. In such a system there will be many very large institutions, some with as many as 50,000 or even 100,000 students. There is likely to be 'open access' for students to higher education. That is to say, while defined entry requirements may persist for some courses, there will be none for many other courses or types of study. Students will be likely to 'drop out' of the system, and many will be working their way through college. Their connection with their institution is likely to be much less formal, in many cases, than is the case in an élite or even a mass system of higher education; a high proportion will be part-time students, and many will be studying by distance learning methods, using programmed learning materials. Because of this more tenuous connection between the student and his institution, and the interrupted pattern of study, course structures will be less firmly defined and are likely to contain a wide range of choice of subject matter. There will be some form of 'credit transfer' system, to facilitate ease of movement for students between institutions as they change their residence, or re-enter the system after a period of full-time work. Because a higher proportion of students will be of mature years, and because most of them will not be seeking to acquire a professional qualification on the basis of apprenticeship to an established scholar in the field, but will rather seek a wide range of technical and 'life' skills, the internal government of institutions will not be dominated by senior academics alone. Students and other teaching staff will be conceded a substantial share in determining what educational offerings are made, and how they are made. At the same time, the sheer size of institutions, and the complexity of running an efficient system of programmed learning, and of credit transfer, will place more power in the hands of professional administrators who will inevitably use management techniques appropriate to very large institutions. All of these features of 'universal' higher education can be observed in North America[6].

Any discussion of the possibility of universal higher education in Britain remains therefore futuristic and academic. In one respect the British system has in the 1970s moved closer to the élite model than before. The reorganization of teacher education means that the old teacher's certificate course, which had a much lower entry requirement than degree courses, is disappearing[7]. The teaching profession represented by the teachers' associations, and notably the National Union of Teachers, saw as a corollary of the recognition of their professional status a steady move towards an all-graduate entry to teaching[8]. But in the British context, obtaining a degree means for all save some mature entrants the acquisition of two GCE 'A' levels by the age of eighteen, or the equivalent thereof. By the end of the 1970s the traditional teacher training route into higher education for those who had failed to achieve this level will have been blocked. The decline in the numbers entering higher education who had not attained two GCE 'A' levels or the equivalent is one reason why the proportion of the eighteen-year old age group 'qualified for and seeking places in higher education' remained static for some years. Another reason may well be that in an élite system the acquisition of a degree is seen as a route into professional, managerial or other superior types of employment, conferring not just higher status, but normally higher earnings as well. By the time that the percentage of eighteen-year olds entering higher education reaches 14 per cent, this syndrome is no longer so apparent since many graduates of the system must take forms of employment hitherto deemed suitable for those with a lower level of educational qualification. Until attitudes towards the relationship of higher education and employment change, there is then likely to be resistance from marginal candidates to the expenditure of time and effort, and the loss of earnings persisting for some years, which are inherent in entry to higher education[9].

One exception to the characterization of the British system as an élite system may appear to be the Open University. This however is dubious. It has some of the characteristics to be found in mass or even universal higher education systems. Thus, its courses are structured on a modular or credit basis. There is a wide range of student choice between course offerings, and those chosen need not necessarily be closely related academically. It is a distance learning system. It can cater for very large numbers of students – by the mid-1970s as many as 60,000 at a time. Interrupted study is not just possible, but common, and most students are in full-time employment. Nevertheless, most Open University students must, despite the existence of some preparatory courses, be prepared to cope with work of normal university level from the outset. The standard of the Open University degree is certainly not lower than that found in other British universities, and is rigorously maintained, not least by the traditional system of external examiners and of external assessors of course material. Because students are of mature years, rather than of immediate post-secondary age, it is possible to argue that the Open University has merely substituted experience and motivation for the more traditional academic entry qualifications. In the 1970s the university operated an 'open access' system, but one that was heavily modified by the pre-counselling of potential students, made possible by the excessive demand over the number of places available[10].

One of the clearest indications of the élitist character of British higher education is the student support system. At first blush this appears generous when compared with that of other countries, where many students have to work their way through college, or incur loans in order to undertake higher education. On the other hand, the mandatory award of a grant to a student in British higher education depends on his acceptance upon a degree course, or the equivalent; or upon a course leading to the Diploma of Higher Education, which is shorter in length but has exactly the same entry requirement; or upon a course leading to qualified teacher status, which as we have seen will presently have the same entry requirements; or finally upon a Higher National Diploma or Higher Technical Diploma course, which are the exceptions to the rule. For the rule is that in general no student of immediate post-secondary age will be accepted upon any of the courses qualifying for a mandatory award unless he has at least five passes in the General Certificate of Education, including at least two at 'A' level. It is true that the 1975 Education Act removed the necessity of prior educational qualifications for mandatory awards, in respect of those who were admitted to full-time degree courses. This provision was deliberately designed to encourage universities and other institutions of higher education to accept upon degree courses mature students who lacked two GCE 'A' levels. Since however there is still no general system of paid educational leave from work, and since the provision applies to full-time degree students only, it can without supplementation never have more than a marginal effect.

It was the same Act of a Labour Government, as amended by the 1976 Education Act, which extended the mandatory award principle to the Higher National Diploma and Higher Technical Diploma courses. Here there is a prior entry qualification, but of a lower level, namely four GCE passes, including one at 'A' level. At the time, there were those working within the policy-making process who saw this extension of the mandatory award principle to those who did not have two GCE 'A' level passes, and were not training specifically to be teachers, as 'the thin edge of the wedge', or embarking upon the descent of a 'slippery slope'. At the time of writing, the wedge remains firmly stuck, and the ice on the slippery slope seems to have melted. There has been no extension of the mandatory principle, and none is in sight[11].

Other students may receive financial support from public sources, but this is at the discretion, both as to whether or not they receive anything, and as to the level of support, of their Local Education Authorities. This applies to all part-time courses of study, including part-time degree courses, whether undertaken at the Open University or elsewhere, and to such part-time courses as the Higher National Certificate and the Higher Technical Certificate. Equally LEA discretion operates in respect of students who are admitted to Diploma of Higher Education courses without the normal educational qualifications, namely two GCE 'A' levels. This is a particularly interesting example, since it might be thought that the introduction of this two-year course of higher education – originally announced by a Conservative Government, but implemented by a Labour Government – might have provided an opportunity to encourage those who had hitherto not succeeded at the highest level in their educational careers, or had dropped out of education at the statutory school-leaving age, to enter higher education, and to proceed if successful to the completion of a degree course. That would have been consistent with a plan to develop from an élitist system of higher education to a mass system. The opportunity was missed, in the name of the maintenance of academic standards, but without doubt partly in order to restrain public expenditure in this area. The Dip.HE therefore offers the possibility of broken study, with progress towards a degree upon resumption, and in some institutions it is used in order to admit to higher education students of mature years whose capacity to cope with a traditional degree course is at the outset in doubt. In the latter case, however, there is no guarantee that the student will be supported from public funds, and few students seem to take advantage of the former possibility[12].

In 1974 the Labour Government agreed to the introduction of a scheme for the payment of the equivalent of mandatory student awards to those mature students who were admitted to courses at the six long-term adult residential colleges – courses which did not of themselves lead to a degree, although in some cases giving exemption from at least the first year of a degree course in the neighbouring University. Prior to this, such students had again been dependent upon the will or whim of their LEAs in respect of financial support. Nearly all such students lack the normal entry qualifications for a degree or other higher education course. Nevertheless, no interest was manifested by government in expanding the number of places available for such students in full-time study, and without paid educational leave, any such effort might have been pointless.[13].

By the late 1970s there existed a complex system of financial support for students who were above the age of compulsory school attendance, but were not in higher education. Some were in receipt of discretionary awards, at a variety of levels, from their LEAs. Others, remaining at school, received maintenance allowances from the LEA – but they were few in number, and the level of such allowances was normally very low.. Others, who had left school, but were unable to obtain work, were able to attend courses at colleges of further education, and still draw the normal social security support offered to non-householders who had not worked and therefore not contributed to the National Insurance scheme (Supplementary Benefit) – provided only that they did not attend instruction for more than three days a week, which was interpreted as being the equivalent of twenty-one hours per week. Others again were enrolled on training, and sometimes further education, courses under the aegis of the Manpower Services Commission. The Youth Opportunities Programme, introduced in 1978, ensured that such young people would receive an allowance of £19·50 per week[14]. The majority of those continuing their education at school, in the hope of entering higher education, or alternatively seeking qualifications in further education, some of which might lead to entry to higher education, received no support from public sources. Despite the announcement in 1978 that the maintenance allowance scheme would be extended, almost certainly at a lower level than some of the rival schemes, this is the clearest evidence that the then Labour Government did not have a policy of encouraging an ever-increasing proportion of young people to remain in education until such time as they had acquired the normal entry qualifica-

158

tions for admission to the higher education system. This structure of financial support is without doubt one reason why the proportion of students in British higher education who were of 'working-class' parentage (that is to say, whose parents belonged to Registrar General's classes C_2DE) never rose above 28 per cent, and by the late 1970s had fallen again to some 24 per cent. Doubtless other factors were at work, but the level of financial support for maintenance and to recompense families for earnings forgone is likely to affect materially the proportion of working-class entrants to higher education[15].

If the system for financial support for students suggests that British higher education remains in essence élitist, that impression is reinforced if we look at the methods of financing higher education institutions and courses, and at the salary structure within the teaching profession. British universities are financed directly by central government, upon the advice of the University Grants Committee, that Committee determining the division of the total sum available between the universities. (The two universities in Northern Ireland are financed by the Northern Ireland Office, which again takes the informal advice of the UGC.) The total sum available for distribution for recurrent grant among the universities is of course determined partly in the light of economic circumstances, but it is related to target student numbers. While the universities encountered some financial difficulty in the mid-1970s because of rapid inflation, the system in normal circumstances guarantees that the provision of finance will be adequate to permit the education of the desired number of students without loss of educational or academic standards[16].

In the non-university sector too there has been in the post-War period deliberate financial encouragement for mounting courses at higher education level. Initially this took the form of a higher level of grant from central government to Local Authorities in respect of such courses. Subsequently, such encouragement was given through the 'pooling' system whereby all higher education courses offered by Local Authority institutions were funded by all Local Education Authorities collectively. While the permission of the Department of Education and Science to mount a new course of higher education in the non-university sector, or continue running a non-economic course, was required, there was clearly here a financial incentive to each individual Local Education Authority and to the institutions which it maintained to substitute, for lower-level work, courses of higher education, as defined in the regulations[17]. Paradoxically, this does not have the effect of translating an élitist system into mass higher education. Because higher education courses impose little direct burden upon an individual Local Authority, whereas the provision of courses leading to acceptable entry qualifications for such courses, as well as the financial support of lower level students, come directly from their own resources, or from those of their immediate neighbours, the system arguably operates in such a way as to cause a bottleneck in the sixteen to nineteen area, blocking off the educational advance of many of those with the potential for higher education.

If this and the pull of status were not enough, the system of remunerating those who teach the post-sixteens reinforces the same tendencies. University teachers have traditionally been paid on scales superior to those operating in the non-university sector. The report of the 1974 Houghton Committee, again established by a Labour Government, sought to remedy this anomaly, and in so doing created another[18]. For some years thereafter there was complaint that those teaching in higher education in the non-university sector were receiving superior treatment to those teaching in the universities. Much less attention was, however, paid to the fact that the Houghton structure continued a grading of work in the non-university sector which ensured that the highest remuneration went to those who were engaged on what was defined as higher education, and that the average level of remuneration obtained by the staff of an institution, or of a faculty or department within it, depended upon the proportion of its work which counted as higher education. Again, the unspoken principle was that higher education should drive out that work the success of which was essential to an increased flow of candidates for admission to higher education. Both this system and the 'pooling' system described in the previous paragraph depend upon restrictive definitions of higher education (Advanced Further Education). Broadly, these definitions correspond to the two 'A' level, or in some cases one 'A' level, entry requirement.

It will be apparent that by embodying in law and practice a narrow definition of higher education, related to prior educational attainment, whether in respect of the payment of staff, or the mode of financing institutions and courses, or the level of public support for the maintenance of students, and by simultaneously building into these three separate systems disincentives for the encouragement of other than academic high-flyers to remain within the education system, successive British governments have inhibited the development of mass higher education. In this respect, Labour governments have been little superior to Conservative governments. Progress towards universal higher education has not yet entered the area of political feasibility.

Officially, the sole underlying philosophy in the development of the higher education system as a whole in the United Kingdom has been the concept of 'social demand', which would be better in this context called 'private demand'. This philosophy was explicitly stated in the Robbins Report[20]. But we have seen that the provision of places for all those qualified for and seeking them, while it appears to be an open-ended commitment to the development of higher education, can operate in a restrictive fashion if the word 'qualified' is narrowly interpreted. For a decade after Robbins, the operation of this principle ensured that the number of places in higher education grew much more rapidly than the Robbins Committee had suggested that it would in its projections of student demand. Thereafter it levelled off, and while by the late 1970s the projections of the Department of Education and Science were based on the assumption that the proportion of the eighteen-year old age group who would fulfil both conditions for entry to higher education would grow slowly to at least 18 per cent, and perhaps 21 per cent, no firm evidence was quoted to justify this assumption[21]. Even if it were to prove justified, the proportion of the population enjoying higher education in Britain would, in default of a sharp increase in the number of mature entrants, remain lower than in many other Western European countries, let alone the United States.

It is possible to question whether the expansion of higher education has been left simply to market forces, as a pure version of the Robbins principle would suggest that it should be. On the one hand, there is little doubt that the majority of university academics in Britain have favoured continued expansion, partly perhaps because of the increased job opportunities it offered to their profession and to them individually, and the increased flow of funds it would bring to their institutions, which on the UGC system of block recurrent grant would include an element for the financing of research as well of teaching. Many have also held that higher education is a desirable end in itself, and should be extended to as wide a proportion of the population as is practicable – although this belief may not always be easily compatible with the unquestioning assumption of many of the same people that academic standards must be rigorously maintained[22]. Academic expansionism marches hand-in-hand with political egalitarianism. The view that investment in education would prove a great social leveller has been strongly held in the Labour Party. By reform of the structure and improvement in the quality of secondary education, the opportunity to achieve well at this level and to proceed to higher education, once restricted in the main to the sons and daughters of professional, managerial, and administrative workers, would be extended to an ever-increasing social range. If broadly similar proportions of the children of all social groups could achieve entry to higher education, then the number of places required would have to grow to a point where the system became one of universal, let alone mass higher education.

161

Part Four: The Political Implications

Such attitudes reflect social and political beliefs, rather than a reliance upon market forces. Nevertheless, by the late 1970s few held them in quite the simple fashion which had been common at the time of Robbins. Experience of financial restriction during the economic recession of the 1970s led many in university circles to doubt whether continued expansion would always be matched by a commensurate increase in funding. More widely, doubts were expressed about whether the quality of secondary education was indeed improving and hence about whether it would provide a greater flow of qualified candidates for higher education[23]. Research in the United States as well as evidence from Britain cast doubt upon the thesis that increased investment in education necessarily produced a higher average level of educational attainment, or equalized life chances among social groups[24]. While such evidence may not have been directly known to most Labour Party members, and while it may not have been totally accepted by all within the senior policy councils of the Party – whom we may define as Ministers directly or indirectly concerned with education, the back-bench group of the Parliamentary Labour Party dealing with education, and the Education and Science Sub-Committee of the National Executive Committee of the Party – it undoubtedly led the latter groups to a more cautious expression of the hopes they placed in increased educational investment. At the same time, recession and Britain's continued poor economic performance had concentrated political attention upon industrial restructuring, measures to alleviate unemployment, and upon the vocational training of a skilled workforce[25]. Investment in education, and in the expansion of higher education specifically, enjoyed a lower political priority than had been the case in the 1960s.

Even in that earlier decade the Wilson Labour Government had manifested some faith in the practicability of manpower planning as a basis for the development of higher education. Such a faith is of course not consistent with reliance upon market forces or private demand. The number of places provided in teacher training and in medical education was overtly determined by manpower considerations[26]. In the former case, because the entry qualification to higher education was lower than that accepted in other sectors, this led to an expansion of opportunities over and above what it would otherwise have been. It is arguable that manpower forecasts are a totally unreliable basis for the development of higher education except in such sectors as these, where the government is the sole or main employer[27]. Nevertheless, even in the mid-1960s repeated attempts were made to forecast the overall demand for scientists and engineers, and for highly-qualified manpower in general. There was concern, which was reiterated by the Callaghan Labour Government, that the inadequacies of British industry were partly the result of a shortage of highly-qualified technical manpower[28]. On this basis, attempts were made to increase the proportion of places in higher education taken by science-based studies, as opposed to arts-based. For the 1967–72 quinquennium the target for the universities embodied a split of places 53:47 in favour of science. The places were provided, but many remained unfilled, because of a shortage of suitably qualified candidates. While a more even target distribution of places was then adopted, complaints about the shortage of science students continued, and the Callaghan government provided cash incentives to attract able students into engineering courses[29].

It is at least doubtful whether there is an overall shortage of scientists and engineers in Britain, although there are certainly bottlenecks in the supply of some types of highly-qualified engineer, and the average quality of science and engineering students continues to give rise for concern. But a mismatch between the pattern of places provided and that of qualified student demand must again act as a restriction upon the growth of the higher education system, in defiance of the Robbins principle. This is seen most powerfully in the university sector, which although 'autonomous', is also as a totality more closely controlled than the non-university sector of higher education. The UGC funds nearly all capital building by the universities. It controls total expenditure on equipment. In allocating block recurrent grant it indicates to universities which of their proposed developments it thinks desirable, and those of which it has taken account in determining each university's grants. While each university remains free to disregard this advice, developments not in accord with the UGC's assessment are likely to be funded only at the cost of other developments. Although there is no firm evidence that the UGC has become increasingly *dirigiste*, as was sometimes suggested, its attempts broadly to steer the development of a much-expanded university system, sometimes in accordance with broad political decisions on the proportion of science-based and arts-based students, or of post-graduates to under-graduates or of overseas students to home students, when combined with conditions of severe economic stringency, undoubtedly mean that the universities as a whole have less flexibility than is sometimes assumed in their pattern of expansion[30]. If then the qualifications of potential students and demand from them do not accord with that pattern, there may be unfilled places in some disciplines and slower growth in others than would otherwise have been possible.

To some degree these constraints are eased by the flexibility of the non-university sector, which is the open-ended part of the system. Here the most powerful institutions are the polytechnics. They were created by the Wilson Labour Government of 1966 specifically in order to be 'socially responsive' institutions – social responsiveness here being defined not as meeting private demand from potential students, but as satisfying the expressed needs of employers and of national and local government. They should seek to meet local need by the provision of part-time as well as full-time courses, and should continue to run 'sandwich' courses, so that some of their students would graduate with employment experience, especially industrial employment experience, as well as having received a formal higher education[31]. Since their establishment some polytechnics have diversified their provision, and there now exist within them non-vocational and arts-based courses. Nevertheless, they remain heavily vocational in orientation, even where the most rapid expansion has been in the field of the social sciences rather than the physical sciences. They have failed to expand their part-time courses, and there are few examples of radical innovation in course structure or the permitted mode of teaching and learning[32]. Some would argue that this is a consequence of the powerful pull exerted by the university model of higher education. It may also be that the Council for National Academic Awards has, in order to assure the academic respectability and acceptability of its own degrees, perhaps discouraged, albeit unconsciously, what are seen as dangerous innovations, normally maintaining for example a requirement for two 'A' level entry.

There have also been physical constraints upon the rate of growth of the polytechnics. In many there persist some inadequacies in specialist teaching accommodation, as well as social, recreational, and library facilities poorer than those found in the universities. There is sometimes an acute shortage of residential accommodation for full-time students. It was unfortunate for them that building programmes were from 1973 onwards severely restricted because of the country's economic difficulties. While this may not materially have affected their capacity to provide for part-time students, it has imposed gross limitations upon the potential rate of growth of some full-time studies in this sector for the foreseeable future. This is one reason why the Callaghan Labour Government, in announcing its plans for the expansion of higher education up to 1981–2, notionally allocated some 55 per cent of all full-time students to the universities in that year [33]. Thus, the universities, with their traditional British approach to higher education – of relatively few mature students, little part-time provision except in respect of post-experience students, unified course structures, and the maintenance of rigid entry qualifications – will continue to dominate higher education. Despite their undoubted success in providing this form of education, and in maintaining high academic standards, this brings no nearer the achievement of mass, let alone universal, higher education.

The re-organization of teacher education which took place in the 1970s, and which arose partly from the desire to achieve an all-graduate entry to the teaching profession and partly because of a rapidly declining birth rate, with as its corollary a commensurate decline in the number of new teachers required, might have afforded the opportunity to broaden the basis of entry to higher education, had conditions been right. But they were not. First, the economic stringency of that period meant that it was inescapable that many of the colleges, especially the smaller colleges, should close, rather than being converted into 'community colleges', offering initial higher education to those with below the normal entry requirement, and acting as 'feeders' for institutions offering degree courses. Indeed, this possibility was scarcely even considered. Although many of the colleges of education were converted to other educational use, Wentworth Castle in Yorkshire becoming, for example, an adult residential college offering many short courses, not least to trade unionists, many effectively ceased to be part of the higher education system.

Secondly, there was available in Britain no course with an entry requirement below that of two GCE 'A' levels which corresponded to the expertise of the teaching staff in most of the former colleges of education, or indeed matched the facilities they had available. Such courses, with for example a one 'A' level entry requirement, exist primarily in technical and business education. These are precisely the fields in which the staff of the former colleges of education were weakest, the colleges themselves usually lacking engineering workshops and laboratories. Those colleges which survived the closures of the 1970s, whether as free-standing institutions or after merger with another college or polytechnic, usually attempted to diversify their provision, mounting courses of 'general' (i.e. non-teacher) higher education alongside teacher education. But for the same reason it was inevitable that the bulk of this diversification should take place in the areas of the arts, social sciences, and the biological sciences. There could therefore be little serious attempt to broaden the entry to higher education, attracting into it substantial numbers of those who had failed to obtain the normal entry requirement by the age of eighteen. At the same time, while some colleges sought to development new course structures, sometimes with a wide range of student choice between the 'modules' offered, with a teacher qualification added subsequently on the consecutive pattern, others opted for the traditional unified degree structure, with professional teacher education given concurrently. This may have been in part a consequence of the desire of many college staff to demonstrate as rapidly as possible their academic respectability, and to secure validation from either a university or the Council for National Academic Awards of their

165

new courses. More traditional courses may be thought more likely to win easy approval than those which are highly innovatory. Difficulties in securing rapid diversification of courses within the colleges were undoubtedly one contributory factor in the Government's decision to allocate to the universities the lion's share of higher education places up to 1981–2.

Some of the colleges of education merged with further education colleges, which offered some courses of higher education alongside less advanced provision. Such colleges have traditionally been one of the growth points of higher education within the British system, advanced courses growing from less advanced. By 1981 there were expected to be 418 non-university institutions offering courses of higher education, many of them part-time courses only [34]. Yet even here there were severe inhibitions on unrestricted growth. Any course at higher education level required the approval of the Regional Advisory Council for further education, and of the Secretary of State, for whom the Regional Staff Inspector of the Department acted. Even when a course was approved and running, it could be cut short by the Regional Staff Inspector if it failed to recruit the required number of students (normally twenty-four in any year). While the control of individual courses, rather than of programmes, does not always optimize the use of resources, some such system of control was perhaps inevitable while higher education in the non-university sector was financed by 'pooling', whereby all local education authorities paid for the specifically higher education provision made by individual authorities. This system is clearly repugnant to normal principles of expenditure control, and successive public committees feared that unless checks were built into the procedure for mounting and running courses, there could be a rapid increase in public expenditure[35].

It was to deal with these and other problems of management and control in the non-university sector that in 1977 there was appointed a working group on the management of higher education in maintained (i.e. public sector) colleges. This is not the place to examine in detail its report (the Oakes Report). We should however note that its recommendations, if implemented, were unlikely to have been expansionist in effect. Some colleges, including without doubt the polytechnics and most if not all of the former colleges of education, would have had their programmes funded primarily by a new National Body. They would thus have been in part subject to a system of control and financing analogous to that operated by the UGC. This of itself would have enabled the Department of Education and Science to exercise a tight control over the total size and cost of the public sector of higher education. At the same time, this control would be reinforced by the continuing role of local education authorities in the proposed system.

They would continue to appoint the governing bodies of most public sector colleges, and would ultimately have to provide 15 per cent on average of their funding. To some authorities this would be a considerable financial burden, and they would have no incentive to permit unrestrained growth within the colleges[36].

Other colleges would, on the Oakes system, receive funding from the National Body only in respect of individual courses, or even on a *per capita* basis for students enrolled on a course. Here again, low enrolment would provide a powerful encouragement to maintaining local education authorities to stop the course in question. Otherwise they might find that they were bearing relatively high costs, in overheads and staff salaries, for the teaching of a small number of students. Initial local authority reaction to the Report was predictably unfavourable[37]. Even if it had not been, it seems unlikely that the Report would have provided a springboard for rapid growth of higher education in the non-university sector. Nothing so far suggests that the Callaghan Labour Government wished greatly to extend participation in higher education. The Labour Party is in any event wedded to the concept of public funding and public control of most, if not all, educational provision. Whatever the merits or demerits of this position, it must in the conditions of the 1970s operate against the rapid development of higher education, simply because there are many competing claimants for a limited amount of public expenditure, and higher education is now perhaps lower on the list of priorities than a decade ago. Within the educational budget itself, some emphasis has been given to the expansion of nursery schooling, and additional funds found for a building programme to ease the transition from selective to comprehensive secondary education. Attempts were made during the 1970s to increase the provision of in-service education and training for teachers, with the objective of having 3 per cent of the teaching force on secondment by 1981–2. A small amount of public money was injected into adult literacy programmes. All of these programmes were seen, whether they were of direct benefit to the less advantaged, or of indirect benefit through an improvement in teaching standards, as tending to the equalization of life chances. While severe economic restraint persisted, it seemed likely that higher education would continue to enjoy a lower priority in the Labour Party than such programmes. While some elements in the Party continued to believe strongly in constantly growing public expenditure, the view of the government was certainly that public expenditure must be tightly controlled in order to permit the individual enjoyment of increased prosperity[38].

On the other hand, the government and the Party were now committed to the further development of sixteen–nineteen education, the emphasis

167

shifting away from the development of early secondary education, where re-organization on comprehensive lines had by 1978 been completed or was nearing completion in most parts of the country. Concern with the sixteen–nineteen group specifically has some of its origins in the historically high levels of youth unemployment in the mid-1970s. This led to the development on an experimental basis of short courses of unified vocational preparation. More significantly, it also led, initially through separate job creation, work experience, and training schemes to a new Youth Opportunities Programme, beginning in 1978. This programme, administered and funded through the Manpower Services Commission, rather than through the Department of Education and Science and the local education authorities, included many elements with little specific educational content. But in addition to the day-release of some of those on job creation projects, the programme also made provision for training schemes which included a substantial element of further education, undertaken at colleges of further education. Some participants in the programme could be sent for full-time study at such colleges. Not only was the programme likely of itself to increase participation in continuing education by sixteen- to nineteen-year olds, but, because it included the provision of a standard allowance, initially £19·50 a week, to all those enrolled in it, it strengthened the case of those who had urged that there should be an educational maintenance allowance or grant for all those remaining in full-time education after the age of compulsory school attendance. This had indeed been a common theme in Labour Party educational thinking for many years, but it was not until 1978 that the Secretary of State was able to announce that a general scheme of means tested allowances for the age group would operate from September 1979[39].

At the same time, there were repeated calls from within the Labour movement, not least from the Trades Union Congress, for a commission of enquiry into sixteen–nineteen education and training. The TUC remained committed, as it had long been, to compulsory day-release to education for all young workers, but again it seems likely that it was the high level of youth unemployment, together with the problem of matching the skills of young people entering the labour market to its changing and more sophisticated demands, that concentrated attention upon this age group[40]. In this context we should note the changing character of the Trades Union Congress, once dominated by the traditional manual Trades Unions, representing unskilled, semi-skilled, craft, and clerical workers. By the late 1970s a substantial proportion of white-collar workers belonged to trades unions affiliated to the TUC, and all the major educational trades unions were affiliated to it[41]. The process began with the affiliation of the Association of Teachers in Technical Institutions (now the National

Association of Teachers in Further and Higher Education) on the 1 January 1967, and culminated ten years later with the affiliation of the Association of University Teachers. It is therefore reasonable to expect that the extension of educational opportunity upwards will in the future rank higher among TUC priorities. Certainly, increased participation in education by sixteen- to nineteen-year olds must lead in the long run to an increase in the level of demand for higher education also.

This may have been one reason why the Callaghan Labour Government, in its discussion document 'Higher Education into the 1990s', published in 1978, assumed as the basis of its central projection of student numbers in higher education a rise in qualified demand to 18 per cent of the age group by the early 1990s. Another undoubtedly was that in the 1970s fertility rates had remained higher among professional and administrative workers ('the middle class') than among manual workers; since the bulk of demand for higher education had historically come from precisely these social groups, it was reasonable to expect that a higher proportion of the total age group would seek entry to it. The high projection used in that document assumed an increase in demand to 21 per cent of the age-group, and the low projection a very modest increase to only 15 per cent. On all projections a steep drop in the numbers entering higher education, in default of other policy changes, seemed likely at the end of the 1980s, in consequence of the decline of the size of the total eighteen-year old age group. On the central projection, this would mean that the absolute number of full-time and sandwich students in higher education would rise from the 1977–8 figure of 520,000 to about 600,000 in 1984–5, stabilising at that level for some six years, and then by 1994 falling back to only 530,000[42].

It was the problem occasioned by such a potential 'hump' in qualified demand for higher education that led to the issue of the document, which is primarily concerned to set out possible policy options for coping with it or eliminating it. Those merely coping with the problem – such as reducing opportunity for those qualified for higher education to enter it in the peak period, or allowing staff student ratios to deteriorate, or renting rather than building new accommodation, or substituting two-year courses for three-year ones, or deferring the entry to higher education of some students in the peak years – need not concern us here. They are all based on the assumption that Britain will not by the end of this century progress far into the area of 'mass' higher education, remaining far short of 'universal' higher education. One set of policy options is however of more interest. Here the document suggested that the number of places in higher education should be kept at least constant at the level of the peak years. This would be done by encouraging, from the end of the 1980s, increased participation in higher education by the children of manual workers, and by providing more systematic opportunities for recurrent education for mature students[43].

It may perhaps seem ironic that the former possibility is canvassed in a document issued by a Labour government as a means of filling some twelve years hence places in higher education that would otherwise remain empty, or alternatively as a means of avoiding a restriction of opportunities to enter higher education in an earlier period. The nearest the document comes to making a political, social, and educational case for encouraging the participation level of children of manual workers to approach more closely that of children of non-manual workers is when it speaks of 'taking positive steps as a matter of social policy'. It suggests that participation rates will be 'as much affected by the gathering impact of policies in the field of housing, health and the social services generally as by educational policies' and that a comprehensive re-organization of secondary schooling means that 'no children will be educated in institutions which, by their status, nature and organization, are apt to cut off their pupils from higher education opportunities'[44]. The latter phenomenon is of course itself the result of past and present educational policies. For there is no discussion here of new policies which might encourage participation in higher education by children from poor homes, or by 'less able' or more slowly developing young people – such as maintenance allowances for the post-sixteens, the creation of community colleges to bridge the gap between the end of schooling and the inception of higher education, new course structures in further and higher education allowing eclectic and broken patterns of study, new modes of assessment of potential, taking account of experience as well as academic achievement or, at the extreme, open entry to higher education for at least a limited period.

As to the second possibility, that of recurrent education for mature students, the document suggests that 'priority might be given at first to those who had missed higher education opportunities at normal entry age'. Such a policy would certainly increase the proportion of the population who benefited from higher education. But the document says that the prospect of a systematic scheme for continuing education at advanced level and at a less advanced level for those in employment 'needs to be viewed in the perspective of continuous social, economic and technological change, which may demand more emphasis on continued education, and may be accompanied by changes in patterns of employment or unemployment', and that such policies would clearly be of concern to the TUC and to the Confederation of British Industry[45]. That is right: but it is a confession that in 1978 there was in Britain, as in most other countries, no long-term strategy welding together industrial, employment, social, and educational policies.

In a country where there is a large measure of open-entry to higher education, and broken study is permitted, and part-time study may be interfused with full-time, with success in a loosely structured amalgam of studies leading to academic award, it may be possible to dispense with such a strategy. In a country where these possibilities scarcely exist, and higher education is almost entirely publicly financed, and its total size tightly controlled, it is not possible.

We must note that the document asks one question of great significance, namely 'what would be the implications of any changes in the present pattern of higher education for the structure of student awards and of higher education courses and qualifications[46]? It does not however, provide much guidance as to its answer. It may be argued that a pattern of recurrent education, at any level, demands both a national system of paid educational leave from employment, and financial entitlements, building up over time, for both the employed and the non-employed, who include such groups as housewives and the severely disabled as well as those who are, strictly-speaking, unemployed. Consideration must also be given to the introduction of student loans for mature students wishing to improve their qualifications, and for those of normal student age who wish to take post-graduate courses or second first-degree courses for which no mandatory award is available, as well as to the support of those between the statutory school-leaving age and the age of entry to higher education and those who are admitted to courses other than those leading directly to a degree without the hitherto requisite prior educational qualifications. If the proportion of the population entering higher education is substantially to increase, entry qualifications must at least be so varied as to encourage the more substantial development of bridging courses for those who have not been in continuous education up to the age of eighteen, and take account of knowledge and skills acquired other than through formal educational channels. This should be possible for full-time as well as for part-time courses, as in the Open University. On the pattern of that institution's provision, course structures must more widely permit the acquisition of credits towards a qualification over a period of years, continuous or discontinuous. That of itself implies permitting a wider mix of studies to count towards the final qualification. It must also be possible to mix modes of study, including 'independent study'. There is nothing radical about these ideas. Most of them have been familiar in the United States for many years; apart from the Open University, there has been relatively little experimentation in Britain[47].

Also essential to any system of higher education which is significantly concerned with 'mass' provision, let alone 'universal' provision, is credit transfer. The document 'Higher Education into the 1990s' does not mention this. On the other hand, by 1978 Ministers in the Department of Education and Science were well aware of the problem and were encouraging the development of credit transfer systems in Britain. The Open University and the Council for National Academic Awards had already concluded an agreement permitting some transfer of credit between the OU and those public sector institutions of higher education which offered CNAA courses, but the universities in general seemed unwilling to enter this system. An efficient system of credit transfer requires an information bank recording the details of courses offered, including their level and content. In Britain no such comprehensive bank existed, but there was a publicly-funded research project into the possibility of establishing one. It is reasonable to conclude that some Labour Ministers were aware of the problems in the transition from élite to mass higher education at least. Yet fragmentation of political thinking within the Party on such matters is well demonstrated by the decision within the same period by the Northern Ireland Department to cease public funding of the Educational Guidance Service for Adults, Northern Ireland, an independent though subsidized body which had over ten years built up the nucleus of such an information bank with regard to the province at least[48].

When in office the Labour Party proceeds in the development of educational policies by a process of 'disjointed incrementalism' – and in the 1970s partly by decrementalism too[49]. In higher education, because of the effect of inherited and traditional structures of institutions and courses, such a mode of policy making has severe limitations, and it may well be that Britain is nearing the point when substantial further advance will demand a radical review and recasting of much of what exists, rather than mere additions at the margin to it. Out of office, the Party recognizes this more clearly. Thus, in 1972 its major policy document said:

> ... in expanding the traditional institutions of higher education, we shall ensure that they too make a contribution to opportunities for those who are not qualified in traditional terms. For this purpose we shall plan places for at least a million full-time students in 1980 with comparable provision for part-timers. ... We shall discuss with the local authorities, the University Grants Committee and the voluntary bodies, the establishment of regional councils to co-ordinate the contribution of all institutions to the comprehensive provision of opportunity. ... We accept the principle that there should be no discrimination in the support given to students by some notion of academic status. ... It is our intention to extend the mandatory grants system to those on courses below degree level and to those,

including mature students, on part-time courses[50].

In another document published in January 1973 a study group of the Party proposed the abolition of existing divisions between further, higher, and adult education by the incorporation of all of them into a new sector to be called simply 'Adult Education'. It criticized the assumption made hitherto 'that the present structure of school education and the existing structure of post-school education will remain unchanged and that no attempt will be made to increase the availability of higher education of some form to students not formally qualified in terms of Advanced Level GCE'[51]. Yet by February 1974, when a general election was upon it, the Party could find no place for higher education in its manifesto, although it did speak of 'a big expansion of educational facilities for sixteen–eighteen year olds'[52]. The combination of economic crisis and of an election after which the Party might again find itself holding the reins of power had a sobering effect.

While the Labour Government remained in power, the disjunction between governmental statements and those inspired by Party activists continued. The former remained sober. Thus, the report of the TUC-Labour Party Liaison Committee in July 1977 – which, because of the involvement of the Prime Minister and other senior Ministers, may be regarded as tantamount to a government statement – again made no mention of higher education. It did however speak of 'giving encouragement to more young people to remain in full-time education by the provision of mandatory educational maintenance allowances'[53]. This of itself would doubtless have the effect of increasing demand for higher education, but the document did not draw that implication.

By contrast, Labour's Programme 1976, published a year earlier, was much more forthcoming. Its educational section was undoubtedly the work of the Science and Education Sub-Committee of the Party's National Executive Committee – and again the thinking of the Party activists who served upon it inspired it. In discussing education after eighteen, the document recognized 'a need to extend educational services to those whose needs are not met by traditional adult education. ... This will mean an involvement not only of the traditional adult educational agencies but also of other groups active in the community, particularly at local level'. Higher education should cater for many of these new adult students, and demand for it should no longer be calculated primarily by reference to the size of the eighteen-year old age group. It was envisaged that there should be 'a national network of interlocking courses and qualifications, which can be taken part-time or full-time to meet the student's personal circumstances'.

There should be progress towards the integration of education and training, and the introduction of a national system of allowances to support students, apparently of any age. Finally, 'discussions should be held with the appropriate bodies in higher education to establish more appropriate entrance requirements for adult students ... and a greater diversity of part-time courses'[54].

Clearly the group which produced this section of the Party's programme was attempting to come to grips with some of the essential prerequisites of extended education and training for all, and of a system of mass and perhaps of universal higher education growing out of it: financial support for all post-sixteen learners, new administrative structures, a diversity of entry requirements for higher education, and mixed modes of study. The distinction between the views of the Government and of study groups established by the Party is scarcely to be sought in the split between the 'left wing' and the 'right wing' of the Party so beloved of cruder political commentators. The membership of the 1973 study group was predominantly right wing or centrist, and the published names of members of the 1976 Science and Education Sub-Committee of the National Executive Committee show no strong left-wing bias[55]. The explanation lies partly in the need felt by Government to act and speak 'responsibly'; some of the Party's proposals would have had a significant price-tag attached to them, and the immediate practical measures required to implement them are not always clear. More important still, Cabinets contain few Ministers whose primary interest lies in post-sixteen education; Party groups studying the subject consist almost wholly of practitioners or ex-practitioners in the field. The British system of government makes it likely that in the development of higher education policy the thinking of Party activists shall often appear idealistic, and that of governments to lack imagination and foresight.

Some Party activists interested in education undoubtedly remained radical in their views, despite (and perhaps partially because of) the economic difficulties of the 1970s. Sometimes they succeeded in gaining acceptance by Party Conference of resolutions embodying proposals for fundamental change. An example is the section of Labour's Programme 1976 which we have just examined. Again, in 1977 the Conference called for:

> ... the urgent preparation of a long-term comprehensive programme under one department of State to provide improved education, training and retraining for the post-school age groups and a higher priority for the continuing education of adults, to include: ... a total review of the financial provisions to ensure equality for young people

and between the generations, and paid educational leave as of right for working people; ... The Government to insist that colleges, universities and local authorities take immediate action towards positive discrimination in favour of the disadvantaged by, for instance, extending admissions criteria to take into account the relative social and educational disadvantage applicants have suffered and by giving more second-chance opportunities[56].

Here again we find reference to some of the keys to achieving a dramatic expansion of the proportion of the population enjoying higher education, such as paid educational leave for all in work and a revision of excessively formal and rigorous admission requirements. But while Party Conference determines the Party's programme, it does not necessarily change the short-term policies of Labour Governments. Nor is the passage of a resolution by Conference a sure indicator of widespread and strong interest in its content within the Party as a whole; it may show primarily that its terms were not objectionable to any powerful group within the Party[57].

One explanation of this disjunction between wider Party and Government interest in the continued expansion of higher education, and that of some Party activists, is that the Party as a whole has become increasingly preoccupied with economic matters in the crisis of the 1970s. Yet economic considerations, above all those affecting employment may in the long run have more influence on the Party than educational theory. The level of educational qualification demanded by the labour market seems to be rising, while the overall demand for labour is likely to decrease, because of technological change. It is probable therefore that the concept of paid educational leave will eventually bulk large in trade union thinking, as it already has in more advanced countries[58]. By 1978 the TUC was already able to say that 'the right to paid release is crucial in any real extension of educational opportunity' and to call for 'a more general debate on the need to make wider provision of paid educational leave available for all adult students'[59]. Developing trade union interest in paid educational leave (PEL) must lead the Party to a serious commitment to a recurrent pattern of learning for adults, much of it at the higher education level.

The structure of the political control of higher education will also be important in any further progression towards universal higher education in Britain. Local control of an increasing proportion of higher education, to which many in the Party are wedded, is sharply to be distinguished from the concept of 'social responsiveness', although the two have often been linked in Labour thinking[60]. Localized control, which was at the heart of the Oakes Committee's remit, may on the one hand mean greater sensitivity

175

to local needs, and greater vulnerability to organized local pressure and demand. On the other hand, it is also likely, if the present financial structure of local government persists, to lead to greater concern about the local impact of the financial demands of higher education. This circle can only be squared if means are found of making higher education available to the bulk of the population at a much lower unit cost than has operated historically. This is perhaps the key to the conversion of more Labour Party activists at local level to the concept of universal higher education, and through them the conversion of future Labour governments.

This points clearly to the need to concentrate upon the development of part-time and mixed modes of study, and equally to the much wider use of packaged learning materials. Here the Open University, itself the creation of a Labour government, has provided valuable experience. It is not however a perfect model. In a system where broken study, credit accumulation, and credit transfer are the norm rather than the exception, a course requiring 320 hours of study for the achievement of one credit – the Open University pattern – is far too long[61]. Prepackaged learning material, whether written or audio-visual, must be produced in much smaller units, for assembly by the student himself, under the guidance of his academic supervisor. The widespread use of such materials in colleges as well in home study should, with very large numbers taking higher education courses at any one moment, produce significant cost reductions when compared with the traditional lecture/tutorial method of teaching. With the use of such methods, as well as of the availability of a wide range of information through the linking of television and telephone systems, home study at post-secondary level becomes practicable for a much wider range of the population than those who have so far shown an interest in the Open University[62]. It then becomes one of those modes of study which students may mix with more official and formal modes in order to progress to higher education qualifications.

The practicability and the economics of such a system are, like some of the other possibilities raised earlier in this chapter – open access, more moderate changes in admissions criteria, broken study, and credit transfer – technical questions which spill beyond the expertise of the traditional educationist. Equally they are not part of the ground covered by normal party political thinking. Labour Party doctrine, formulated in a less technological age, sees only a steady extension of opportunities for traditional modes of study to those who were in the past excluded from them. Most Labour Party activists have little conception of the possibilities for greatly extending higher education through such means, let alone having thought through the practicalities of doing this. Granted therefore that the system of higher education in Britain has been geared to the education of an élite, and that most party political thinking is bounded by the horizons of that élitest system, the prospect of establishing universal higher education in Britain seems at present no more rosy under Labour than under Conservative administrations. Only increasing unemployment, and an ever greater mismatch between the skills of the workforce and the demands of the economy, are likely to drive Governments into investing resources in the development of post-secondary education to an extent which will make more likely progress towards universal higher education in the United Kingdom.

Notes

[1] Detailed British statistics will be found in:
   i) *Higher Education* (1963), Appendix Two (A).
   ii) Layard R., King J. and Moser C. (1969).
   iii) *Student Numbers in Higher Education in England and Wales* (1970).
   iv) *Higher Education into the 1990s* (1978).

There are difficulties in the definition of courses of higher education in the United Kingdom. Such courses have a terminal standard above that of General Certificate of Education 'A' level, or the equivalent. They will normally have an entry requirement of 4 or 5 GCE passes, with 1 or 2 at 'A' level. But the Teacher's Certificate has no 'A' level requirement.

[2] *Vid.* Trow M.A. (1970 and 1973). For the general argument of the following paragraphs cf. McConnell T.R. and Berdahl R.O. (1971) and Fowler G.T. (1971). International comparisons are made in Cerych L. and Furth D.E. (1972).

[3] In January 1978 it was announced that the proportion of the post-school age group entering higher education was expected by the Government to rise from about 13 per cent in 1977–8 to about $14\frac{1}{2}$ per cent in 1981–2. The distribution of students was intended to be, in the latter year, 310,000 in universities and 250,000 on higher education courses at other institutions: 'The Government's Expenditure Plans 1978–9 to 1981–2' (1978), vol. II, p. 78, para. 12.

[4] The degree by independent study was introduced at North-East London Polytechnic. On this, modular degrees, and interdisciplinarity, *vid.* Burgess T. (1977), cap. 4, and cf. Owens G. and Soule L. (1978).

[5] The recasting of governing bodies and academic boards in institutions of higher education began with the 'Report of the Study Group on the Government of Colleges of Education' (1966). It continued with the issue by DES of 'Notes for Guidance' (1967) on the government and organization of polytechnics; the Education (No. 2) Act 1968, giving effect to the recommendations of the 1966 Report; the concordat made between the Committee of Vice-Chancellors and Principals and the National Union of Students in 1969, introducing student representation to university Councils; and DES Circular 7/70, extending junior staff and student representation to the government of further education colleges other than polytechnics.

[6] *Vid.* Trow M.A. (1970 and 1973), and with the argument of this paragraph cf. Turner C. (1977), p. 8.

[7] The Minister of State at DES announced on 27 July 1978 that the last intake to the old Teacher's Certificate course would be in September 1979. The change was foreshadowed in *Education: A Framework for Expansion* (1972), paras. 73–81, and confirmed in *Eduction in Schools: a Consultative Document* (1977), para. 6.11.

[8] *Vid.* Gosden P.H.J.H. (1972), pp. 305–310. The first step towards conceding all-graduate entry was agreement on the elimination from teaching of those who were not fully trained: Schools (Qualified Teachers) Regulations (1969).

[9] This tentative conclusion might be drawn from the results of an enquiry conducted by the Office of Population Censuses and Surveys in collaboration with Professor Gareth Williams and Alan Gordon of Lancaster University, of which an outline was published in 'Reports on Education No. 86' (1976).

[10] On the demand for entry to the Open University *vid*. Sir Walter Perry (1976), cap. 9, and esp. p. 145 Table 4, which reveals that 61·8 per cent (1971) of entrants, falling to 52·4 per cent (1975) were 'qualified' for higher education in the sense of already having two GCE 'A' levels or the equivalent.

[11] The argument of this paragraph rests on unpublished evidence. The Government intended to introduce mandatory means-tested maintenance allowances for sixteen- to nineteen-year olds still in education, as from September 1979; but that is not the same as an extension of mandatory student awards.

[12] The theory of the new DipHE course was set out in *Education: A Framework for Expansion* (1972), paras. 110–113. There were subsequent hints that the two 'A' level requirement might not be immutable; e.g. the then Minister of State at DES, speaking at Birmingham on 30 January 1976, said: 'I think the general requirement for a two 'A' level entry will have to be maintained for at least a while but I would not want to be inflexible about this nor, I think, do the validating bodies.'

[13] *Adult Education: A Plan for Development* (1973), paras. 251 and 255.2 proposed that a new adult residential college should be opened in the northern half of England, and thanks to local initiative the former Wentworth Castle College of Education in Yorkshire was subsequently converted to this purpose. But Fircroft College, Birmingham, one of the six existing long-term adult residential colleges, closed its doors because of student and staff difficulties in 1975. Note that automatic grants for unqualified adult students come close to the American concept of 'financial entitlements' for adults: vid. Kurland N.D. (ed.) (1977).

[14] *Young People and Work* (1977) recommended an allowance of £16 per week, plus £2 per week standard travel allowance, but inflation necessitated an increase in the total allowance to £19·50 when the new Programme was introduced on 1 April 1978. By contrast, the average maintenance allowance awarded by LEAs in 1975 was £2·22 per week. Conditions for entitlement to supplementary benefit are set out in Administrative Memorandum 4/77 (1977) and Amendment No. 1 to it (1978).

[15] Cf. n. 9 *supra*. In 1978 the Trades Union Congress said: 'It has long been known that the proportion of young people from working class homes who go on to higher education is and always has been severely restricted': *Priorities in Continuing Education* (1978), p. 9.

[16] The most succinct account of the working of the UGC system in the 1970s is to be found in *Policy Making in the Department of Education and Science* (1976), pp. 325–46.

[17] The administration and financing of the public sector of higher education is described in

Report of the Working Group on the Management of Higher Education in the Maintained Sector (1978), cap. II, pp. 2–7; cf. Regan D.E. (1977), caps. IX and X, and Cantor L.M. and Roberts I.F. (1972), cap. 2.

[18] *Report of the Committee of Inquiry into the Pay of Non-University Teachers* (1974), cap. 5.

[19] 'Higher education' is in Britain a term of art (vid. n. 1 supra). 'Advanced Further Education' more accurately describes those FE courses with a terminal standard above that of GCE 'A' level, although not all 'advanced' courses are also 'poolable'.

[20] *Higher Education* (1963), cap. VI.

[21] *Higher Education into the 1990s* (1978), para. 5 and Appendix II.

[22] *Vid.* Halsey A.H. and Trow M.A. (1971), esp. cap. 11.

[23] The best evidence for this proposition comes from the so-called 'Great Debate' of 1976–7. *Vid.* esp. the speech of the Prime Minister at Ruskin College, Oxford, 18 October 1976, reported in *Times Educational Supplement* (1976), and 'The Attainments of the School-Leaver' (1977). The general concern about standards in education apparent in the mid-1970s is analysed in Fowler G.T., The Politics of Education, in Bernbaum G. (ed.) 1979.

[24] For Britain *vid. The Attainments of the School-Leaver* (1977), and cf. Baldwin R.W. (1975). The best American summation of the research is Jencks C. *et al.* (1972).

[25] *Vid. Towards a Comprehensive Manpower Policy* (1976), as well as *Young People and Work* (1977).

[26] Ahamad B., in Ahamad B. and Blaug M. (ed.) (1973), caps. 10 and 11. Useful evidence for the basis of forecasting the requirement for teachers is provided in 'Reports on Education No. 85' (1976) and 'No. 92, (1978), on the future size of the school population. For medical education *vid.* esp. *Report of the Royal Commission on Medical Education 1965–8* (1968).

[27] Despite the views expressed by the sometime Minister of State at DES, Lord Crowther-Hunt, in the *Times Higher Education Supplement* (1976) and elsewhere, *vid.* Merrison A.W. (1975) and *Policy-Making in the Department of Education and Science* (1976), p. 345, Q. 1112.

[28] Evidence from the 1960s can be found in:
   i) *The Brain Drain* (1967).
   ii) *Enquiry into the Flow of Candidates in Science and Technology into Higher Education* (1968).
   iii) *The Flow into Employment of Scientists, Engineers and Technologists* (1968).
For the 1970s *vid. Industry, Education and Management* (1977), which discussed the need for technically competent managers; and the speech of the Prime Minister at Ruskin College, n. 23 *supra*, where mention was made of unfilled science and technology places in higher education.

[29] *University-Industry Relations* (1977), paras 25–28, cf. 5–24. The intention to award 100 National Engineering Scholarships worth £500 p.a. tax-free was announced by DES on 22 May 1978.

[30] *Vid.* n. 16 *supra*.

[31] Speech of the Secretary of State for Education and Science, the Rt.Hon. C.A.R. Crosland,

at Woolwich Polytechnic, 27 April 1965 (the source of the phrase 'socially responsive'), and 'A Plan for Polytechnics and Other Colleges' (1966).

[32] *Vid*. n. 4 *supra*.

[33] *Vid*. n. 3 *supra*.

[34] *Report of the Working Group on the Management of Higher Education in the Maintained Sector* (1978), p. 63, Appendix B.

[35] *Further and Higher Education* (1972), paras. 48–55; and *Local Government Finance* (1976), cap. 7, paras. 24–28.

[36] *Report of the Working Group on the Management of Higher Education in the Maintained Sector* (1978), paras. 5.1–4, 5.9, 5.26–29, 7.7–16, 7.26.

[37] *Ibid*., paras. 7.4–7.6. For the maneuvring of the local authority associations, *vid*. e.g. the *Times Higher Education Supplement* (1978).

[38] *Vid*. 'The Government's Expenditure Plans 1978–79 to 1981–82' (1978), vol. I, para. 2: ' . . . in order to leave room for manoeuvre on taxation, it is necessary that the planned growth rate for total public expenditure should be within the prospective growth rate of national income.' Cf. para. 65: 'The public expenditure plans described in this White Paper should permit a sustained improvement in standards, while allowing at the same time a substantial growth in personal consumption after four years of no growth.' The indications of economic policy here given were realized in the 1978 Budget.

[39] 'Parliamentary Debates' (1978), vol. 949 'Written Questions' col. 617, and vol. 950 'Oral Questions' col. 227–9. It seemed likely that the full allowance under the scheme would be below the level of single non-householder supplementary benefit.

[40] *Priorities in Continuing Education* (1978), pp. 3–4; cf. *The Next Three Years and Into the Eighties* (1977), p. 7, paras. 16–18.

[41] The process leading to the affiliation of the ATTI, the National Association of Schoolmasters and the National Union of Teachers is analysed in Coates R.D. (1972), cap. 8.

[42] *Higher Education into the 1990s* (1978), paras. 5 and 9, and Appendix II.

[43] *Ibid*., paras. 30–34.

[44] *Ibid*., para. 32.

[45] *Ibid*., paras. 33–34.

[46] *Ibid*., para. 37 (xiii).

[47] But *vid*. n. 4 *supra*.

[48] DES appointed a Steering Committee for the Credit Transfer Information Centre research project in 1977, and research began at the end of January 1978. Public funding of the EGSA in N. Ireland ceased two months later.

[49] For 'disjointed incrementalism' *vid*. Braybrooke D. and Lindblom C.E. (1963), and for decrementalism in the 1970s, Fowler G.T. in Bernbaum G. (ed.) 1979.

[50] *Labour's Programme for Britain* (1972), pp. 58–59.

[51] *Higher and Further Education* (1973), pp. 20 and 22.

[52] *The Labour Party Manifesto 1974* (1974), p. 12.

[53] *The Next Three Years and Into the Eighties* (1977), p. 13, para. 37.

[54] *Labour's Programme for Britain* (1976), pp. 85–86.

[55] Six of the eleven members of the 1973 Study Group were MPs, ex-MPs or peers, all from the right or centre of the Party. Some of those who served on the 1976 Sub-Committee were published in the *Times Higher Education Supplement* (1976), pp. 1 and 28.

[56] *Report of the Seventy-Sixth Annual Conference of the Labour Party* (1977), pp. 283–295.

[57] In the short debate on this Resolution, five speakers from the floor discussed it, including the mover, the seconder and the present author; only one was a trade union delegate. Six speakers in the same debate preferred to discuss a Resolution on nursery education; three were trade union delegates. For the relationship between the political ideas of party activists and the policies of the party leadership, *vid.* Rose R. in Rose R. (ed.) (1969), pp. 368–390; and Rose R. (1974), pp. 198–217.

[58] e.g., the Swedish legislation of 1975 on PEL owed much to trade union pressure.

[59] *Priorities in Continuing Education* (1978), p. 10.

[60] *Vid.* n. 31 *supra*.

[61] The Open University 'credit' is roughly the equivalent of six months successful full-time study at a conventional institution of higher education: *vid.* Sir Walter Perry (1976), pp. 60–75.

[62] *Vid.* e.g. Milner E., in Houghton V. and Richardson K. (ed.) (1974), pp. 71–79.

References

Official Publications

Administrative Memorandum (DES) 4/77 (1977), London, DES; and Amendment No. 1 to Administrative Memorandum (DES) 4/77 (1978), London, DES.
Adult Education: A Plan for Development (1973), Report by a Committee of Inquiry appointed by the Secretary of State for Education and Science under the Chairmanship of Sir Lionel Russell CBE, London, HMSO (*The Russell Report*).
A Plan for Polytechnics and Other Colleges (1966) (Cmnd. 3006), London, HMSO.
    Circular 7/70 (1970), London, DES.
Education: A Framework for Expansion (1972) (Cmnd. 5174), London, HMSO.
Education in Schools: A Consultative Document (1977) (Cmnd. 6869), London, HMSO.
    Education (no. 2) Act 1968.
Enquiry into the Flow of Candidates in Science and Technology into Higher Education (1968) (Cmnd. 3541), London, HMSO (*The Dainton Report*).
Further and Higher Education (1972), Report from the Expenditure Committee of the House of Commons, Session 1971–72, vol. I (HoC 48-I), London, HMSO.
Higher Education (1963), The Report of the Committee appointed by the Prime Minister under the Chairmanship of Lord Robbins 1961–63 (Cmnd. 2154), London, HMSO (*The*

Robbins Report); and Appendix Two (A) (Cmnd. 2154-II).

Higher Education into the 1990s (1978), A Discussion Document, London, HMSO.

Industry, Education and Management (1977), A Discussion Paper, London, Department of Industry.

Local Government Finance (1976), Report of the Committee of Enquiry (Cmnd. 6453), London, HMSO (*The Layfield Report*).

Notes for Guidance (1967), London, DES.

Parliamentary Debates (1978) (Hansard), House of Commons, Session 1977-78, vols. 949 and 950.

Policy Making in the Department of Education and Science (1976), Tenth Report from the Expenditure Committee of the House of Commons, Session 1975-76, London, HMSO.

Report of the Committee of Inquiry into the Pay of Non-University Teachers (1974) (Cmnd. 5848), London, HMSO (*The Houghton Report*).

Report of the Royal Commission on Medical Education 1965-68 (1968) (Cmnd. 3569), London, HMSO (*The Todd Report*).

Report of the Study Group on the Government of Colleges of Education (1966), London, HMSO (*The Weaver Report 1966*).

Report of the Working Group on the Management of Higher Education in the Maintained Sector (1978), London, HMSO (*The Oakes Report*). (Cmnd. 7130).

Reports on Education No. 85 (1976). *The Future School Population*, London, HMSO.

Reports on Education No. 86 (1976), *16 and 18 Year Olds: Attitudes to Education*, London, HMSO.

Reports on Education No. 92 (1978), *School Population in the 1980s*, London, HMSO.

Schools (Qualified Teachers) Regulations (1969), SI 1969 No. 1777, London, HMSO.

Student Numbers in Higher Education in England and Wales (1970), Education Planning Paper No. 2, London, HMSO.

The Attainments of the School-Leaver (1977), Tenth Report from the Expenditure Committee of the House of Commons, Session 1976-77, HoC Paper 526-I, London, HMSO.

The Brain Drain (1967), Report of the Working Group on Migration (Cmnd 3417), London, HMSO. (*The Jones Report*).

The Flow into Employment of Scientists, Engineers and Technologists (1968) (Cmnd. 3760), London, HMSO (*The Swann Report*).

The Government's Expenditure Plans, 1978-79 to 1981-82 (1978) (Cmnd. 7049), London, HMSO; and vol. II (Cmnd. 7049-II).

Towards a Comprehensive Manpower Policy (1976), London, Manpower Services Commission.

University-Industry Relations (1977), The Government's Reply to the Third Report of the Select Committee on Science and Technology, Session 1975-76 (Cmnd. 6928), London, HMSO.

Young People and Work (1977), London, Manpower Services Commission (*The Holland Report*).

Other Publications

AHAMAD B. and BLAUG M. (ed.) (1973), *The Practice of Manpower Forecasting*, Amsterdam, Elsevier Scientific Publishing Company.

BALDWIN R.W. (1975), *The Great Comprehensive Gamble*, Macclesfield, Helios Press.

BERNBAUM G. (ed.) (1979), *Schooling in Decline*, London, Macmillan.

BRAYBROOKE D. and LINDBLOM C.E. (1963), *A Strategy of Decision: Policy Evaluation as a*

Social Process, New York, Free Press of Glencoe.

BURGESS T. (1977), *Education after School*, Harmondsworth, Penguin.

CANTOR L.M. and ROBERTS I.F. (1972), *Further Education in England and Wales* (2nd. edn.), London and Boston, RKP.

CERYCH L. and FURTH D.E. (1972), *On the Threshold of Mass Higher Education, the World Year Book of Education, 1972–73*, London, Evans.

COATES R.D. (1972), *Teachers' Unions and Interest Group Politics*, Cambridge, CUP.

FOWLER G.T. (1971), *Mass Higher Education in Britain*, The Third Annual Education Lecture Delivered at the University College of Swansea 12 March 1971, Swansea, University College of Swansea.

GOSDEN P.H. J.H. (1972), *The Evolution of a Profession*, Oxford, Basil Blackwell.

HALSEY A.H. and TROW M.A. (1971), *The British Academics*, London, Faber and Faber.

Higher and Further Education (1973), Report of a Labour Party Study Group, London, The Labour Party.

HOUGHTON V. and RICHARDSON K. (ed.) (1974), *Recurrent Education*, London, Ward Lock Educational.

JENCKS C. *et al.* (1972), *Inequality*, New York, Basic Books; reprinted (1973), London, Allen Lane.

KURLAND N.D. (ed.) (1977), *Entitlement Studies*, Washington, The National Institute of Education.

Labour's Programme for Britain (1972), London, The Labour Party.

Labour's Programme for Britain (1976), London, The Labour Party.

LAYARD R., KING J. and MOSER C. (1969), *The Impact of Robbins*, Harmondsworth, Penguin.

McCONNELL T.R. and BERDAHL R.O. (1971), 'Planning Mechanisms for British Transition to Mass Higher Education', *Higher Education Review* Autumn 1971.

MERRISON A.W. (1975), 'The Education of Ministers of State', in *Universities Quarterly*, vol. 30 no. 1, Winter 1975, London, Turnstile Press.

OWENS G. and SOULE L. (1978), *The Module*, Denby Dale, SLD Publications.

PERRY, SIR WALTER (1976), *The Open University*, Milton Keynes, The Open University Press.

Priorities in Continuing Education (1978), London, TUC.

REGAN D.E. (1977), *Local Government and Education*, London, George Allen and Unwin.

Report of the Seventy-Sixth Annual Conference of the Labour Party (1977), London, The Labour Party.

ROSE R. (ed.) (1969), *Studies in British Politics*, (2nd. edn.), London, Macmillan.

ROSE R. (1974), *The Problems of Party Government*, London, Macmillan.

The Next Three Years and Into the Eighties (1977), London, The Labour Party.

The Labour Party Manifesto 1974 (1974), London, The Labour Party.

Times Higher Education Supplement (1976), No. 239, 21 May 1976, London, Times Newspapers Ltd. and (1978), no. 351, 4 August 1978.

Times Educational Supplement (1976), no. 3203, 22 October 1976, London, Times Newspapers Ltd.

TROW M.A. (1970), 'Reflections on the Transition from Mass to Universal Higher Education', *Daedalus*, Winter 1970.

TROW M.A. (1973), *Problems in the Transition from Elite to Mass Higher Education*, Carnegie Commission on Higher Education, New York, McGraw Hill.

TURNER C. (1977), in *Educational Administration* Spring 1977, The Journal of the British Educational Administration Society, Blagdon, BEAS.

PART FIVE

Conclusion

10. Open Admissions and Numerus Clausus – Causes and Consequences

Torsten Husén

The German magazine *Der Spiegel* in 1976 (No 25) ran a feature article with the title *Numerus clausus: Ende des Unsinns* (Numerus clausus: the end of nonsense). Elections to the *Bundestag* coming up in the fall of 1976, politicians on both left and right pledged to abolish *numerus clausus* which had been introduced some years earlier in order to control the enrolment explosion at the German universities. According to the German constitution, everybody who has passed the secondary school leaving examination, the *Abitur*, is entitled to a place of study at a university. Since in most programmes there were more applicants than places available, a selection had to take place within certain set *numerus clausus* quota. A federal agency for the allocation of places of study has been set up in Dortmund with a computer-based selection and allocation procedure.

If the balance between number of places available and the number of applicants has been upset in a country like the Federal Republic of Germany, where until recently a relatively modest proportion of young people in the relevant age bracket had their university entrance qualification examination and where still this examination is a necessary prerequisite for university entrance, the situation has in certain respects become even more critical in other countries, where a policy of open admissions not only for secondary school leavers at large but for adults with work experience and certain minimum academic qualifications as well has begun to be implemented. Interestingly enough we invariably find that in countries where the admissions requirement has been liberalized that sooner or later financial, logistic, and other restraints have forced the government to consider some kind of selective rank ordering of applicants. Quite a lot of imagination has been mobilized in deciding upon criteria of selection and categorization of applicants.

I shall first deal with the causes behind the policies of broadening access to what until now has been called higher education but more appropriately should be labelled tertiary or post-secondary education. (Whether in the future it would be justified to talk about higher education shall not be discussed here. But evidently it begs the question: Higher than what?)

Then I shall deal with the ensuring dilemmas that almost universally

187

beset tertiary education in the highly industrialized countries and the institutional strains associated with these dilemmas.

Finally, I shall discuss some solutions that would have to be contemplated in order to cope with the present dilemmas and institutional strains.

The 'revolution of rising expectations'

What the economists liked to refer to as 'social demand' for education has increased tremendously because of three circumstances. In the first place, extended provisions for formal schooling, particularly at the secondary level, tend to speed up participation rate and expectations for further-going education. Secondly, enhanced standards of living among the broad masses are conducive to demand for more education that is seen as a vehicle for upward social mobility and increased pecuniary benefits. Thirdly, the Western world has since the early 1960s been infused by a high-powered political rhetoric on equality and justice.

By the end of the Second World War the great majority of young people in Western Europe had a mandatory schooling that lasted between six and eight years, as a rule provided in the elementary school. At that time already the majority of young people in the age range fourteen to eighteen went to secondary school in the United States. In conjunction with reforms of the structure of the systems, secondary education began to become universal in Western Europe in the 1950s and 1960s. The broadening of opportunities profoundly affected the educational aspirations in social strata where a few years of elementary schooling traditionally had been the only provision for those destined for manual occupations. The phenomenon of successive 'shock wave' effects has been studied by sociologists in both capitalist and socialist countries (Husén, 1974). Enrolment explosion at one level will with some time-lag touch off an explosion at the next higher level, unless particular measures are taken to restrict enrolment. The process can also be observed in several developing countries, such as Ghana and Kenya.

Enhanced standard of living has as one consequence increased 'consumption' of education. We notice also here a certain time-lag. The private automobile tends to appear before the university student in a working-class family (Husén, 1975). The transition from an ascriptive society, where advanced formal education is a prerogative of those who by birth, wealth and connections are designated for leading positions, to a society in which access to and promotion within the educational system formally depends on tested ability was regarded as a tremendous step forward in 'democratizing' education. But the psychological barriers within the social strata, from which young people traditionally did not proceed to higher education, turned out to be stronger than antcipated by those who thought that economic reforms would suffice. Studies in participation rates in higher education conducted for instance by OECD or by the Office of the Chancellor of the Swedish Universities (Gesser and Fasth, 1973) consistently provide evidence that extended provisions for higher education and increased formal accessibility to it have not radically changed the social composition of the enrolment. Those people who tend to take advantage of increased opportunities are already in favoured positions or from relatively good social background; some consistently tend to be more equal than others.

The most important factor behind the 'revolution of rising expectations' has been the quest for equality and justice. Since the 1960s the Western world has been obsessed with what I would like to call an egalitarian euphoria. Talent, irrespective of geographical location, ethnic background, social origin, and economic means should be given the opportunity to become developed. Benefits would thereby accrue both to the individual and to his country (Husén, 1974). The egalitarians focused mainly on equality *between* groups. Blacks were compared with Whites, and working-class youngsters were compared with middle- or upper-middle-class youngsters, whereas inequalities *within* groups attracted much less attention both among policy makers and researchers.

The very concept of equality has become considerably widened. The old liberal doctrine that everybody should have an equal chance to make it to the top, to which general lip-service always has been paid, was considered not to be enough. The goal was not equality of *opportunity* but equality of *results*. A 'redemptive' egalitarianism has entered the scene (Husén, 1975).

The idea of equality of opportunity some ten to twenty years ago gained strong momentum, when in most Europen countries still a very select social and intellectual élite of some three to ten per cent of the relevant age groups went on to higher education. There was evidently a considerable untapped 'reserve of talent' in lower social strata which was shown by comprehensive surveys in countries such as the Federal Republic of Germany, Sweden, Austria, and France. Corresponding surveys had been conducted in the United States, where participation rates in higher education were much higher than in Europe. The most famous of these studies was Dael Wolfle's *America's Resources of Specialized Talent* (1954). At the end of the 1950s, economists began to evaluate talent in terms of wealth of nations (see, e.g., Harbison, 1973). The egalitarian philosophy turned out to be a strong ferment in the reform of national educational systems at a time when the need for highly-trained manpower seemed almost insatiable and when social demand for education inspired expanded provisions of advanced formal education.

The enrolment explosion in higher education has in the 1960s been more intensive in Europe than in the United States, where the expansion at both the secondary and tertiary level has been more gradual since it has taken place over a longer period. In a paper for the Hiroshima International Seminar on Higher Education in April 1976, I presented some figures on the startling expansion of higher education in the Netherlands, Sweden, and the United Kingdom (Husén, 1977). The financial implications have been staggering, such as an eight-fold increase in constant prices of the operating costs in the Netherlands in less than 25 years. Costs have soared in a similar way in other countries.

However, in the long run the planning strategy of 'life-long' or 'recurrent' education will perhaps in some European countries become more important than the increase of secondary school leavers who go to higher education. Within the framework of such a strategy post-secondary provisions will become available to an increasing proportion of both young people of regular university age and adults who have been working some years and who intend to alternate between study and work. Post-secondary provisions, to a large extent consisting of job-oriented courses, are made available to adults at any point in their careers. For example, within the framework of the 'dimensioneering' of the total number of places of study envisaged by the U68 Commission in the new system of post-secondary education in Sweden, a certain number of places are set aside within the various programmes and courses for adults with work experience and limited academic qualifications. This means that according to the new regulations of admission young people of regular university age will not compete with adults for places. Each category has been assigned its own quota of places according to the number of applicants of the respective categories (Husén, 1977).

The utilization of institutions of higher learning for recurrent education is an attempt to realize the social ideal of increased equality of options during the career of an individual. It should be left to him when and how he wants to take advantage of publicly financed education. Recurrent education thus becomes what somebody has referred to as an 'emancipatory strategy' that will provide the individual with the tools he needs in order to shape his life.

It should be pointed out that the new policy in Europe of widening access to post-secondary education for both students who go straight from school to university and for adults who have been in working life for some years has led to the introduction of entirely new criteria of admission, such as work experience and age.

Dilemmas besetting admissions policy

Evidently, a comprehensive system that in principle proclaims open admission for all secondary school leavers, and in addition is promising working adults that they could enhance their career prospects by intermittently taking university courses covering the whole range from traditional academic hard-core study to vocational skills, is due to face certain troublesome dilemmas. I shall here deal with three of them:

1. Aspirations for post-secondary education versus restrained financial and logistic resources. This dilemma is particularly prevalent in studies requiring high-level teaching staff and expensive technical facilities, such as medicine and engineering.

2. Excellence versus equality. There are certain aspects of the policy of equality that are not compatible with criteria of excellence. This was the reason why excellence versus equality was chosen as the main theme for the Third International Congress of Higher Education at the University of Lancaster 1975. At the bottom of this is the more fundamental dilemma between equality and meritocracy.

3. Self-fulfilment in advanced studies versus the demand on the part of society for the 'production' of due quotas of 'brain workers'. The U68 reform of higher education in Sweden was strongly resented by the students not least because the entire system of courses was so explicitly job-oriented.

The 'revolution of rising expectations' has led to a staggering rise in costs for higher education. Various checks on such a development could be conceived. Admissions restrictions could be imposed, be they called *numerus clausus* or not. In a society where a small intellectual and/or social élite proceeded to higher education, there was with few exceptions a balance between number of places and number of applicants. But for a long time in many European countries entry to certain professional programmes, such as medicine or civil engineering, has been locked. The school leaving examinations administered by the secondary school provided a uniform entrance ticket to the university.

Even in a doctrinal egalitarian society, such as the Swedish, the Commission on Higher Education (U68) had to acknowledge that provisions of higher education would have to be offered within the framework of what they euphemistically refer to as 'total dimensioneering'. In case there are more applicants than study places available a selection has to take place. The ceiling set on intake depends not only on restricted financial resources but is a step to avoid 'over-production' of highly educated manpower.

It is interesting to note how one has gone about reconciling on the one side openness and equality with restraints and selection on the other. The applicants are divided into groups – quotas – which are given a number of places according to their relative size.

The reconciliation between equality on the one hand and restraints such as finance on the other has been achieved by employing different sets of criteria or by weighting these criteria differently within the various categories of applicants. By adding age as a criterion one tries to safeguard that those who have their formal schooling at a time of limited opportunities will not be too handicapped in competing for entry with the young people who have just graduated from secondary school. Work experience is another criterion serving the same purpose. But in order to guarantee each category of applicants a certain share of the total number of study places available, each applicant competes only *within* his own category: youngsters fresh from secondary school with their age-mates and adults with a minimum number of years of work experience with other adults. Thereby a certain balance between various categories is achieved.

But what allegedly aims at bringing about more equality and justice between groups can easily create glaring inequalities or injustices in individual cases. For instance, it has occurred that applicants (successfully) have suppressed academic credentials in favour of work and age credentials in order to be allocated to a category where the chances are greater to be admitted to a tertiary programme. It is in my view somewhat disconcerting to find that institutions whose purpose is to promote academic excellence and where success in studies by all empirical evidence is reasonably well predicted by academic criteria counteract that purpose by an access policy biased against academic excellence.

The Swedish system of getting access to higher education, which in some respects might seem extreme, typifies present trends in the provision of access in several countries outside the East European hemisphere. In the latter, working experience has long since been used as a criterion of admission. In the first place certain non-academic criteria, such as age and amount of work experience, are used along with school marks and scholastic aptitude test scores. Furthermore, the applicants are categorized and eventually compete within their own categories. In a strictly vocationally-oriented system of courses the weighing together of various types of qualifications can to a certain extent claim to be rational. But when it comes to more advanced study in a given discipline, age and work experience can no longer as easily be considered along with purely academic merits.

All empirical evidence gathered tells us that selectivity and equality are by no means compatible. Particularly selectivity on the basis of academic criteria can hardly be reconciled with equality of access and even less with equality of results. (Husén, 1975). Those who are most likely to succeed in such a system are those who have the advantage of a stimulating home background.

The plight of tertiary education of our days is that the ever rising aspirations for such education everywhere tend to outdistance the capacity of our delivery system. Thus, even if the relative share given to higher education of the total public resources increases we shall for the foreseeable future have to live with certain measures taken in order to accommodate a limited number of students from various categories, i.e. some kind of *numerus clausus*. In addition we can envisage deep-going institutional changes in order to achieve such an optimization. I shall come back to this at the end of this paper.

I agree with a statement made by Edward Shils at the Lancaster Conference 1975 on higher education, that excellence and equality are by no means mutually exclusive (Shils, 1975). The change from an élite to a mass higher education does not necessarily lead to 'more means worse' in terms of the average standard of those admitted. In the United States where data on IQ and scholastic aptitude test scores are available over a considerable period, one finds that up to a certain point, opening the system has not lowered the average intellectual quality of the admitted, most likely because the change has implied the tapping of resources from other social strata than those who traditionally have been recruited to the universities. (Taubman and Wales, 1973).

Expanded enrolment almost invariably means increased spread of performance. Then the crucial problem, which not least the excellence-oriented European universities have experienced recently, becomes *what segment of the enrolment is going to set the standard*. As long as the top segment is the standard-setter, those with inadequate preparation or without conspicuous intellectual interest (who in earlier days were those ending up with the gentleman's B grade) act only as somewhat cumbersome ballast. But if they are allowed to set the standard two essential tasks of the universities are in jeopardy. In the first place, they tend to slip out of their role as centres of intellectual inspiration and pursuit. Secondly, they will increasingly find it harder to pursue their role as centres of basic research, a task which, traditionally, they are the only institutions in society to fulfil.

In a critical analysis of the Swedish reform of higher education I have tried to analyse the tensions between the research system and the system designed to produce 'brain workers' according to certain quotas and specifications (Husén, 1976). The dilemma that many universities face in the era of mass higher education is the preservation of the union between teaching at the undergraduate level and research. This dilemma is strongly felt not least in Europe, where the massification and manpower orientation of

193

programmes have occurred more abruptly than in the United States where there has been a tradition of pragmatism in higher education since the passing of the Morrill Act in the 1860s.

Inspired by ideas about manpower planning and scared by recent imbalances between the number of graduates and places available that traditionally have been occupied by such graduates, recent European reforms have reflected a tendency to orient programmes towards job sectors and specific jobs within these sectors. It has been a pleasant day dream among many top bureaucrats, for instance in Sweden, to devise a system in which intake of students and labour-market demand are perfectly matched. Reforms to this effect have however been strongly resisted by both students and professors. The resistance also shows an interesting political alliance between traditional conservatives and the new left, whereas the establishment represented by the central government, business, industry, and labour unions have been in favour of such reforms. At the core of resistance against such a system is the aspiration among an intellectually qualified minority (or is it even a majority?) of students that university attendance is not only a preparation for a particular slot in life but also a period of self-exploration and self-fulfilment. To these students the essential aspect of university is not the credit-giving machinery or the acquisition of formal credentials but the opening up of new vistas, and attempts to come to grips with one's own role in life. A young German professor (Fischer, 1973) with leanings toward neo-Marxism after having followed the Swedish U68 commission on higher education went home and wrote a book with the title *Die Produktion von Kopfarbeitern* (The Production of Brain Workers). He had an important point.

How do we resolve the dilemmas and incompatibilities created by the open admissions policy and the ensuing massification of higher education? Evidently, as is illustrated by the German case, locked studies or *numerus clausus* with an elaborate system of selection is not a solution in the long run. Radical institutional changes would have to be contemplated in order to avoid deleterious effects on the rest of the educational system both below and above the undergraduate level.

Comprehensivization of secondary education which qualifies for some kind of higher education becomes imperative. This has already been implemented in, for instance, the United States, whereas in leading European countries selection for university-preparing secondary education still takes place at the age of ten to twelve.

Tertiary education will have to be diversified or differentiated both in terms of programmes and the intellectual demands they pose and in terms of entrance age to these programmes. By diversifying and vocationalizing tertiary programmes, to which access is granted from all kinds of secondary school tracks, the pressure (*Leistungsdruck*) is taken off secondary education. At the same time the pressure for entry is alleviated. A system of recurrent education, in which the individual can chose the time for his re-entry into the system, widens the range of options during his life career. Recurrent education has, as mentioned above, been referred to as an 'emancipatory strategy' which frees the individual from the bonds of his background and environment and makes it easier for him to acquire at various junctures the tools he needs in order to shape his life. It would not any longer be necessary to aspire to an optimum amount of formal education at an early stage of life in order to make the best out of one's potentiality.

Universalization of upper secondary education, open admissions to tertiary education, diversification and comprehensivization of teaching by including programmes that previously were not in the university domain, the introduction of short-cycle programmes have all in a way blurred the line of demarcation between what was previously considered to be two very distinct domains, secondary and higher education.

Finally, higher education faces, under the auspices of massification and narrow vocationalization, an unavoidable dilemma. Scholarly pursuits germane to a university easily come into conflict with a system of courses designed to provide very specific vocational skills and competence. The scholarly pursuits, particularly that of basic research, are by definition reserved for a select few, even if many feel that they are called. My point is that these diverse activities cannot with success be conducted within the shell of a cafeteria-designed institution for mass consumption.

In a recent article (Husén 1976–7), based on a comprehensive critical review of the reform of the Swedish university system (Husén, 1975), I have tried to advance a rationale for allocating undergraduate education with a clear vocational thrust to separate tertiary schools, where the institutional organization would serve this aim alone and not try to contribute to the extension of the knowledge base which traditionally has been associated with higher education. The limited sector of higher education made up of researchers and graduate students could then carry on their work at institutions (of moderate size) serving a more clear-cut purpose. The functions vested in the 'research universities' would be to pursue basic research and to train prospective researchers as well as teaching staff for the post-secondary system. Such a differentiation is something quite new in Europe, where until recently the universities have all been élite institutions and therefore more easily could combine high-level undergraduate teaching with research and graduate studies. In the United States, élite institutions already at the undergraduate level can recruit young people with primary interests in intellectual endeavours and who are material for graduate studies and other advanced pursuits.

Bibliography

BERGENDAL, GUNNAR (1977) *Higher Education and Manpower Planning in Sweden*. Stockholm: The National Board of Universities and Colleges.

BERDIE, R. *et al*. (1962) *Who Goes to College?* Comparisons of Minnesota College Freshmen, 1930–60, Minneapolis: University of Minnesota Press.

FISCHER, LUDWIG (1973) *Die Produktion von Kopfarbeitern*. Berlin: VSA.

GESSER, B. and FASTH E. (1973) *Gymnasieutbildning och social skiktning* (Upper Secondary Education and Social Stratification). Stockholm: Office of the Chancellor of the Swedish Universities.

HARBISON, FREDERICH H. (1973) *Human Resources as the Wealth of Nations*. London: Oxford University Press.

HUSÉN, TORSTEN (1974) *Talent, Equality and Meritocracy*. The Hague: Martinus Nijhoff.

HUSÉN, TORSTEN (1975) *Social Influences on Educational Attainment*. Paris: Organisation for Economic Co-Operation and Development (also in French and German).

HUSÉN, TORSTEN (1976–7) 'Swedish University Research at the Crossroads', *Minerva*, vol. 14:4, 419–446.

HUSÉN, TORSTEN (1977) 'Access to Mass Higher Education' in *Perspectives for the Future System of Higher Education*. Hiroshima, Japan: Hiroshima University.

SHILS, EDWARD (1975) *Discovery, Excellence and Equality in Higher Education*. Third International Conference on Higher Education at the University of Lancaster, 1–5 September 1975.

TAUBMAN, P. and WALES T. (1973) *Mental Ability and Higher Educational Attainment in the Twentieth Century*. A Technical Report prepared for the Carnegie Commission on Higher Education. Berkeley, California: Carnegie Commission on Higher Education.

Contributors

Gordon Roderick Welshman. Head of the Division of Continuing Education at the University of Sheffield. Professor of Adult Education.

Michael Stephens Cornishman. Robert Peers Professor of Adult Education and Dean of the Faculty of Education at Nottingham University.

Kenneth Lawson Assistant Director of the Department of Adult Education at Nottingham University. Oxford-trained philosopher. Author *Philosophical Concepts and Values in Adult Education.*

Geoffrey Sims Vice-Chancellor, University of Sheffield. Former Deputy Vice-Chancellor at Southampton University. Distinguished engineer.

Bernard Crick Professor of Politics and Head of the Department of Politics and Sociology at Birkbeck College, London University. He was President of the Politics Association from 1969 to 1976. Numerous publications in the area of politics and education.

Robert Houlton Chief Education Officer of the National Co-operative Education Association and Principal of the Co-operative College. Former BBC producer – economist at Liverpool University.

Colin Fletcher Senior Research Officer within the Faculty of Education at Nottingham University. Author of a number of books within the field of sociology. Poet and Merseysider.

Gareth Williams Professor of Educational Planning at Lancaster University. A well known Cambridge-trained writer and authority on higher education.

Alan Maynard Senior Lecturer within the Department of Economics and Related Studies at York University and a distinguished contributor to the field of the economics of education.

Keith Hampson M.P, former lecturer in American History at Edinburgh University. He studied at Bristol University and in America at Harvard and was Personal Assistant to Mr Edward Heath in 1968.

Gerry Fowler Professor Associate of Government at Brunel University. Formerly Labour Member of Parliament for The Wrekin and three times Minister of State for Education and formerly Professor of Educational Administration at the Open University. Distinguished writer and commentator on education.

Torsten Husén Head of the Institute of International Education at Stockholm University. Chairman of a number of international committees for such agencies as UNESCO and the writer of some of the best known pieces in the field of educational thought.

INDEX

Index

201

Index

Index

Index

Stigler, G. 121, 122, 127
St. John-Stevas, N. 151
Stoikov, V. 103, 111
student drop-out 102, 104
student unions 135, 148, 155, 177

Taubman, P. 126, 127
Taubman, P. and Wales, T. 193, 196
Tawney, R.H. 117, 127
teacher training 40, 62, 155, 163, 165–167
Technical Education Act (1889) 134
Thatcher, Rt. Hon. Mrs. M. 14, 151
Thompson, B. and Beggs, A. 94, 95
Tocqueville 59
TOPS Programme 147
Trade Union Congress (TUC) 77, 84, 142, 168, 169, 170, 173, 175, 178, 183
trade unions 83, 168
  shop stewards 75–81
  teacher unions 121, 155, 168–169
Training Services Agency (TSA) 142
Trow, M.A. 101, 102, 103, 111, 113, 127, 151, 153, 177, 183 (*see also Halsey and Trow*)
Tullock. G. 122, 128
Turner, C. 177, 183

UNESCO 12, 111
United States Congress 9
'Universal' higher education
  British lag in 23
  constraints 160, 169, 177
  costs of 13, 22, 99–111, 112–127
  cost/benefit 103–106
  demand for 109–110
  lack of incentives 132
  need for 19, 86
  need for diversity of institutions 110
  need for 'rationing' 109–110
  political implications 21, 30–31, 55–72, 93, 131–150, 153–177
  problems of definition 27–30, 100–101, 112–114
  as recurrent education 103
  required conditions for 102

resistance to 13
universities
  comprehensivisation 27
  control of 163
  development of 37–39, 42, 137
  extra-mural departments 17, 38, 41, 53, 61, 75
  as 'ivory towers' 32, 38, 43, 52, 54, 62, 65, 135
  objectives of 11–12
  responsiveness of 10, 39, 134, 138, 140, 175 (*see also Open University*)
University Grants Committee (UGC) 139, 148, 159, 161, 163, 166, 172
University of Athens 75
University of Hull 17
University of Liverpool 75

Vernon, G. (*see Flint et al.*)
Verry, D. and Davies, B. 124, 128
vocational skills development 9–10, 12–13, 17–18, 32–34, 44–45, 48, 50–53, 83, 86, 104–105, 113, 141, 144, 146, 155

Wales, T. (*see Taubman and Wales*)
Walker, A. (*see Maynard and Walker*)
Warnock, M. 28, 35, 117, 128
Weaver, Sir Toby 21
Wellings, A. (*see Bacon et al.*)
Wells, J.H. (*see Flint et al.*)
Williams, G.L. 103, 111, 119, 197
Williams, G.L. and Gordon, A. 178
Williams, Shirley 12
Wilson, Sir Harold 133
Wiltshire, H.C. and Mee, G. 94, 95
Wofle, D. 189
Woodhall, M. and Vernon 124
Woodhall, M. and Ward, V. 128
Workers Educational Association (WEA) 70, 90
Working-men's Club and Institute Union 84

Youth Opportunities Programme 158, 168

206